EVERYTHING YOU NEED TO KNOW ABOUT GRANTS

EVERYTHING YOU NEED TO KNOW ABOUT GRANTS

HOW TO WRITE THE GRANT—HOW TO GET THE GRANT—WHERE TO GET THE GRANT

Business Development Sourcebook

ANTHONY HOLLIS

iUniverse, Inc.
New York Lincoln Shanghai

EVERYTHING YOU NEED TO KNOW ABOUT GRANTS
HOW TO WRITE THE GRANT—HOW TO GET THE GRANT— WHERE TO GET THE GRANT

iUniverse, Inc.

For information address:

iUniverse, Inc.
2021 Pine Lake Road, Suite 100
Lincoln, NE 68512
www.iuniverse.com

First Edition

Unless otherwise noted, all Scriptures have been taken from the King James Version of the Bible.

ISBN: 0-595-33821-6

Printed in the United States of America

This book is dedicated to my dear wonderful wife, Nicole, who has loved and stood by me these 10 years. You never stopped caring for and helping me. You deserve to have this first major publication breakthrough dedicated to you.

To my dear children Jasmine, Peachlyn, Khalif and Kolby, who sacrificed many hours of their "special time" together with their dad during the writing of this book.

2000 PLUS GRANTS AND FUNDING ORGANIZATIONS

Grants for Computers and Technology Programs

Grants for Religion and Social Change

Grants for Schools and Educational Programs

Grants for Business and Economic Development

Grants for Affordable Housing Programs

Grants for Minorities

Grants for Elderly Programs

Grants for Children and Youth Programs

Grants for Community Development Projects

Grants from Government Agencies

Grants for Development of Homeless Programs

Grants for Health Care

Grants for the Disabled

Grants for Recreational Projects

◆ Nonprofit Organizations   ◆ Ministries   ◆ Community Agencies

CONTENTS

SECTION I

HOW TO WRITE THE GRANT

SECTION II
HOW TO GET THE GRANT

SECTION III
WHERE TO GET THE GRANT

THE BUSINESSPERSON'S 23RD PSALM

The Lord is my mentor

I shall not flounder.

He shows me where opportunities lie.

He leads me to safe havens.

He restores my hope.

Though I walk through the

Valley of disappointment,

danger and despair,

I will fear no failure

For He is with me.

His expert direction and training

Brings me security.

He presents my greatest lessons

In the midst of the chaos around me.

He affirms my personal worth

And I'm filled with confidence.

Surely growth and maturity will mark my life

All the days we are associated.

And I will be His friend and partner forever.

SECTION I

How to write the Grant

ENCOURAGING WORDS

"And the Lord answered me, and said,
Write the vision, and make it plain upon tables,
that he may run that readeth it."
(Habakkuk 2:2)

ENCOURAGING WORDS

So you have a great idea that stretches your organization past its' comfort zone, but you have no funding to back it up. You constantly hear that there are billions of free dollars that go unclaimed each year in the form of grants, but you don't know how to go about obtaining these grants. What do you do? Where do you go? Who do you reach out to, to help make your vision a reality?

You attempt to raise funds in your congregation or organization, but you receive little to no response. You even attempt to write grant proposals but you find the process too confusing or unfruitful. While you want to carry out the vision that has been entrusted into your hands by God, questions and concerns begin to mount in your mind; you experience feelings of frustration, you become overwhelmed and anxious and ultimately you give up. **Has this ever happened to you?**

Although you may have heard that grants are plentiful and easy to obtain; truthfully speaking, there is a science to writing grants and obtaining funding. There are strategies that have to be implemented in order for organizations to successfully receive repeated funding. Grant writing is more than picking up a directory and looking up donors and writing an "essay". Grant writing is a strategic, well-organized, fact finding document that not only demonstrates a need in the community but gives concrete support showing that your organization is capable of fulfilling that need. Grant writing is not a mystery or a myth. Grants are obtainable.

I would first like to say thank you for allowing our company to serve your organization and become a part of the solution that your organization is addressing in your local community or region. What a wonderful opportunity it is to be part of a great move. In the time that I have worked with various nonprofits, churches, businesses, and various entities; I have personally seen miracles happen before the eyes of many because of organizations, like your own, receiving grant monies. I have watched God perform many miracles and have seen lives changed.

I am sure that for you, as for many of us, with every new level and initiative that you take in faith, you will meet a level of resistance. We both know and understand that this is to be expected and we must equip ourselves with the necessary tools that it takes to make this happen. Your vision shall come to pass and I truly believe with knowledge and the right equipment, we will be able to transfer wealth into the hands of people who will effectively transform their communities.

The purchase of this book tells me that you are ready to be one of those persons who are ready to make an impact on this dying world. As we all take a look at the current situations in the world, we must begin to answer the plaguing questions that face us.

- ✍ Who would have thought that there would be six-year-olds taking armed weapons to elementary schools to shoot their classmates and school-teachers?

- ✍ Who would have thought that a 12-year old child would stand in front of a judge, facing life in prison and not shed a tear?

- ✍ Who would have thought that educated mothers would have to feed their children from dumpsters as they sleep on park benches night after night due to lay-offs and cutbacks?

- ✍ Who would've thought that seemingly innocent men would beat their girlfriends and wives until they were not recognizable?

Who would've thought? No One! But the reality is, that this and far worse is happening in our world today and this is why organizations like yours is needed. We must seize this opportunity to reach out, assist in changing lives, and make a difference.

So many people are waiting on the other side for us and just as their lives are valuable to God, they are valuable to us. Through grant funding, we have the opportunity to offer programs, services, housing, jobs, training, and much, much more to these unknown persons. I know that we can make a difference. As you begin to read on, learn and apply the necessary skills to acquire grant funding, *"Being confident of this very thing, that He which hath begun a good work in you will perform it until the day of Jesus Christ"* **Philippians 1:6.**

INTRODUCTION

"Wisdom is the principal thing therefore get wisdom:
and with all thy getting get understanding"
(Proverbs 4:7)

INTRODUCTION

First, let's begin by defining what a grant is? According to Webster's dictionary, a grant is a gift for a particular purpose. Expounding on this definition, I would venture to say that a grant is an act of transferring funds from a funding agency to a petitioner seeking funding for a specific purpose whose main goal is to carry out that purpose while serving a targeted group of individuals.

Grants are revenue-generating vehicles used to fund service-providing agencies or organizations that, under normal circumstances, have limited resources available to them for a particular program or project. The majority of grants are awarded to IRS identified 501(c) 3 tax-exempt organizations. More information on 501(c) 3 tax-exempt status is available in the next chapter.

If you are a start-up church or nonprofit organization, your first grant may come in the form of seed money. Seed money is for a grassroots' organizations that either do not have a program in place or the organization is beginning to seek outside money for the first time. Grants are made available to institutions, individuals, public and private agencies, community organizations, and nonprofit agencies around the world. Grant funding sources include federal, state, county, city, cdc, corporate, foundations, individuals, and fundraising campaigns.

Grants are based on performance and how well your agency can carry out the proposed project. The most common misconception among organizations is that when a grant is awarded, you can do what you want to do with the money. That is totally incorrect. You must do what you said, in your proposal, you would do. A grant does not equate to a free money gift or shopping spree, you must be good stewards over the money that is granted to you. Continual grant awards are contingent upon you performing your intended objectives.

Grants have within them implied accountability. Grants are awarded based on a number of factors. These factors include goals and objectives, needs, uniqueness, budget details, demonstrated ability to carry out your project, support, measurable outcomes, and evaluations. You must have a realistic expectation for achievement. Furthermore, future funding is riding on past performance. Before grant recipients are chosen, grantors assess the feasibility of each proposal. There are times when an organization's proposal is too ambitious, (i.e. "Our organization is going to feed 100,000 people in 3 months with $25,000) and therefore, not awarded. The funding agency sees that the organization is setting unrealistic goals. One of the most important steps is to articulate reasonable goals that can be measured in a meaningful way. Your goals should be what you can realistically do. Don't make your goals too abstract and grandiose. Once your goals are set, you should identify a cost-effective way to measure progress.

Grant competition is fierce and you must follow the grantor's guidelines to the letter. You must keep in mind that the actual grant writing process is just one step in the grant-seeking process.

Start by writing **a concise, focused, bulleted statement of your project's specific goals**: who, what, when, where, why & how much. Limit it to [1] one page each for: (a) your project description and goals, (b) action plan/implementation timetable and (c) a detailed line item budget &/cash flow. Then ask ten qualified friends to read it. If it doesn't make sense to them without additional explanation—it won't make sense to the funder!

How are you going to **assess and measure community needs** and then involve **all of your project stakeholders** (board, staff, clients, and other agencies) in telling your story and marketing your project—to the larger community? Public meetings, hearings, seminars, workshops, and surveys are usual methods.

How will those needing services find you? How can the community support you if you keep it a secret? A good project-marketing plan reflects broad-based community involvement, research, documentation, participation, education and support—from the get go!

Good ideas alone—do not make a grant! Grant makers often tell us that they have no dearth of good ideas...**they lack of a realistic measurable implementation plan** that often gets in the way. A well-defined and measured need, clear goals, detailed budget plus time-based and measurable objectives, are critical to obtaining funding.

How are you going to measure your success? You'll need achievable goals and program scope, time-based (incremental) & measurable objectives). What will you do when, step by step, by what date[s]? Don't wait until the end of the grant to see if you got it right! **Realistic, incremental, monthly and quarterly, quantitative _and_ qualitative benchmarks are very important.**

This is not the Grant maker's first rodeo. Many projects have been brought to the table before you got there. Over time, Grant makers develop exceptional skill detecting and evaluating projects that are likely to work and those that may be fatally flawed. **Try not to overstate your case, or your deliverables.** *Smoke and mirrors have a very limited audience.* Better to deliver more than expected and projected than struggle to achieve impossible objectives—like **climbing Mount Everest alone—without oxygen!**

Grant makers know and understand that **real, <u>sustained</u> community transformation takes time—and lots of very tough, often frustrating, and persistent hard work.** You'll want to celebrate your incremental achievements, and report on them as you go along.

Telling a wonderful story—but failing to request a specific amount—doesn't work! You can help the Grant maker help you…by being open, clear, concise, well organized, and focused. **Grant makers don't have a crystal ball to read your mind, they just want to help.** Assume nothing, and provide clear focused answers to anticipated questions!

Requesting a specific amount—without clearly justifying its realistic use or specific intended measurable purpose(s)—guarantees rejection. **The phrase "Just give me the money and I'll figure out what to do with it later" is a very familiar (and unfunded) request!** It is a recipe for future; reactive, non-profit crisis management…you already have more than enough surprises just making the system work!

So, you'll need complete, realistic, accurate line item budgets and cash-flow projections (current and future) identifying ALL of your sources of income and expense. Your Excel/Lotus spreadsheet, projecting you'll deliver comprehensive services, to thousands of clients on a shoestring budget, in 12 months, will **not** impress a funder.

What will work **is a tough, lean-but-do-able budget that focuses hard-won dollars and broad community support on specific, needed, demonstrated, well documented, well researched, and measurable quantitative (what you will do) and qualitative (how you will do it) unduplicated services.**

Unduplicated counts mean that you count each person you serve—just once—and then individual units of service to that person separately. 500 meals served to 100 participants <u>are not</u> 500 people served. Its five hundred meals served to 100 people! **You <u>must</u> keep very accurate records of costs and units of service delivered,** not only to demonstrate success—but also to project needs and costs accurately next year.

Don't be afraid to ask for what you really need—**within the funding guidelines and limitations of the grant maker**—but be prepared to fully justify it! An under-funded project, (only because you didn't think through what it would really cost beforehand), is a constant distraction from your job of delivering services. If you can also tangibly demonstrate a broad base of shared community involvement, plus real community ownership and participation (cash, in-kind and volunteer involvement)—all the better!

How will your project or services be sustained *after* the grant runs out? The needs you have identified that you want to serve didn't begin with the grant or will they end when the grant runs out! How will you, proactively, as a core element of the project, build a wider donor base of community participation, ownership and investment to gradually take up the load by the end of the first, second or third year funding?

However unpleasant it may seem, **now is the time to think about these downstream funding issues** and build them into your grant application…not reactively, in a panic, weeks before the money runs out!

Funders are reluctant to invest in recreating the wheel, in your community. Do research, use the internet, **Check out what others have done and are doing in your community,** and across the country. Invite them to tell you about their project call them, go visit their project, partner with them. Learn from their mistakes and successes. Funders expect you to know your community and to demonstrate your knowledge in your proposal. Who is doing what? Can you forge a strategic alliance or partnerships?

You need direct, demonstrable, broad-based, community stakeholder collaboration, participation and involvement. **These stakeholders, strategic partners and alliances will help you to reduce costly duplication of effort on devolving and limited funds, very cost-effectively.**

Board & staff: how will you successfully manage the project? Folks who have "Been There—Done That" can help you in the tough times. **A well-trained Board is a great asset!**

You can't do it all yourself—<u>unless burnout is one of your measurable objectives</u>!

If you want a charitable philanthropic contribution—you need to do your legal and accounting homework. **Granters are very specific about what they need.** In many cases, you <u>**will not**</u> be able to obtain corporate or foundation funding without a 501(c) (3) actually in place. Though you may be able to request a planning or capacity building grant, many times you will be required to present as a part of your application, the following:

A copy of your IRS letter of 501(c) (3) determination (your formal nonprofit status) plus your Fed Tax ID #. If you don't know what these are, or simply don't have them, you will need to see a consultant, accountant or an attorney ASAP. DO THIS FIRST—or all your hard work will simply get you a friendly rejection letter that says. "Come back and see us when the 501(c) (3) is actually in place!" You could find an existing 501(c) (3) you can strategically partner with but you must also work within their restraints and requirements.

The IRS nonprofit 501 (c) (3) tax-exempt determinations will take a number of months—so plan on it! The initial several page applications for non-profit tax ID # <u>are not</u> an IRS 501(c) (3) determination. The IRS forms required to complete the 501(c) (3) application are many pages long and (the IRS says—and they are correct) it may take <u>at least 60 hours</u> to complete!

Always remember that <u>N</u>eeds <u>A</u>lways <u>E</u>xceed <u>R</u>esources! You know that you are NEAR the problem but you feel FAR from the resources. How do we get these two ends to meet? You must ask yourself the following question, which needs are you addressing, why and how? What is the long term ROI (<u>R</u>eturn <u>O</u>n the Grant makers <u>I</u>nvestment in your project)? Is it advocacy, change, improved emergency or transitional services, housing, education, innovation, an exhibit, performance, unique collaboration, reduced duplication of services?

What specifically are you going to deliver, to whom, at what cost, to what tangible benefit, over what period of time? Your proposal needs to clearly define each of these objectives and measurable outcomes to be considered for funding.

Is your project specific to your community, and why, could others learn and benefit from or replicate your experience? Funders would love to invest in projects that have broader demonstration grant applicability. (There are, of course, many one time events and unique community needs to be addressed). If you don't have the required funds to get started, or the staff to write grants, consider hiring a consultant or start by writing a small capacity-building grant to fund grant writing or a community needs assessment to get started.

Once you are successful, what is your plan to tell others in the community about your program and services?

As you proceed, how do you plan to document what worked, what didn't—and why? The grant maker and grant seeker are partners in your project. You both have a right and a need to know how it is going each month over the course of the grant—first, because you want to continue—and early problem detection is easier and less costly to correct. Second, Grant makers may want to fund other successful projects—like yours, that work!

Write a bulleted, one page Executive Summary introducing your project, it will help you to present your project's "talking points" locally before you seek funding and will provide you with the opportunity to "work the bugs out of your proposal"…

(Actually, starting your grant seeking process with this strategic mission document will focus your project and your grant maker search.)

Keep it Simple: Plan your Work—Then Work your Plan!

Lighten up—Give your passion and creativity a voice. Grant makers receive hundreds of applications—**but first, they need to get past your first page!** (Also known as **the 30 sec. test!**) This is your opportunity to stand out in the crowd, capture imagination, and invite further in depth review with a clear, innovative focus.

Grant makers want you to be successful! After you receive your grant, keep the Grant maker informed of your progress. However, often the grant or project does not go exactly as planned. You learn from your experience, and may need to adapt, change, or modify your method or approach—en route. **It's a partnership—talk it out—before using the funds for modified uses! It's all about trust.**

We often learn as much about what doesn't work as what does! The **Queen of Denial** doesn't live in Egypt! Community organizational development and service delivery is all about client-centered needs assessment, resource management, strategic planning, hard work, passion, risk, persistence, innovation, collaborating, networking…and lots of listening and learning! Its hard work isn't it?

So, keep the door open, maintain clear open lines of communication, and sustain real trust. You may have another project that needs funding…so **don't burn your bridges.** If you both knew it wouldn't work in the first place, it would not have been funded! Your learning will be valuable to you…and to the grant maker.

Grant makers receive many funding requests for projects and activities that the Grant maker has <u>clearly stated</u> that they do not, cannot, or will not fund. Find out <u>in advance</u> what the Grant makers annual funding priorities and guidelines are **before sending** your proposal out.

Many Grant seekers seem to use a shotgun/email spam approach, send off a dozen copies of a funding application—one to every philanthropic organization that comes to mind. This just wastes paper, postage, both the Grant makers and your valuable time. **This is not a bulk mailing!** Be sure, when you send your foundation cover letter, application or proposal that you address it—if at all possible—attention of or directly to a person with whom you have already talked.

(Idea: This is a partnership—not a lottery!)

It is much better to build a solid partnership with good clear communication, and then send one appropriate, complete proposal to that funder…your funding odds are much better! **NOTE: If you are seeking funds for one project from multiple funders—each taking a piece—then you need to be upfront about all of that, with everyone, from the get go! No games!**

So, down to the wire…**If you have done your careful research and partnership homework—then what the grant maker wants to fund, is able to fund, and (after rigorous review) <u>MAY</u> be willing to fund—will closely match what you propose actually needs to be funded!**

Finally, reality check—even if your application is everything you want it to be—doesn't give you the go ahead to begin spending funds in your organization *as if the grant check is in the mail!* There is very, very stiff competition for grants.

Remember: **Only one out of nine equally qualified proposals get funded.** Keep at it. Be persistent. Broaden your donor base…that's where 90% of the money is! (Download eBase donor management software—it's powerful and its' free to non-profits at http://www.techproject.org/ebase.html)

Find and build strong-shared vision, purpose with community and agency alliances. If your goal is to meet community needs, **you can significantly reduce your competition for grants (and attract more funders) by putting strategic, collaborative project partnerships together—then everyone wins!**

If you don't get funded, don't take it out on the grant maker! Refine your project, your skills and your presentation…**if this was easy, someone else would have done it—before you got there!** Check it out, Ask (don't demand). Funders know you are disappointed, as are the other 90% of the applications who also couldn't be funded—Mark it off to learning. Be persistent. Stay focused. What was missing? How could we have presented it better? What got funded? What can you learn from their project? Be a good detective. Funders favor the prepared!

It is really OK to <u>Ask for Help</u>! You may have to hire a qualified Consultant that has "been there—done that" and they can help you get the job done quickly and efficiently—also, be sure to ask for a clear detailed written proposal…(Just as the Grant makers are asking for one from you!)

NOTE: Anyone who guarantees to get you the grant or the money—if you just pay them in advance is probably not the right person or organization. No consultant can guarantee to get the grants you need, but their time, skill and experience are valuable. Although you may pay upfront fees, a seasoned consultant will write a portion of their fees as a development officer (if allowable) into the grant proposal thereby helping you to recoup some upfront costs.

So, fasten your seat belt, put the funding process into low 4-wheel drive, be persistent, courageous, creative, innovative, collaborative, inclusive of all of your stakeholders and agencies (including your board, staff, clients/your customers)…and stay focused!

It is certainly tough hard work to try to do grant writing and research in the midst of all of the other demands, pressures and time constraints that you have on your plate!

According to Jon Hardie/Maine Circuit Riders Initiative **the grant seeking/grant making process is all about building a partnership. Partnerships are crucial to the success of many projects that your organization desires to be funded.** This careful prospect research, needs and resources analysis by the Grant seeker is **critical**. Taking the time to build a relationship—to build a match, then submit a well thought through and complete application—certainly helps the process work better—for both partners.

As federal funds devolve and decline, there is greater competition for limited foundation resources. As a result, Grant makers are swamped with inappropriate proposals. **80% of foundations have <u>no</u> staff.** The net effect is to overwhelm funders with paperwork and delay decisions for legitimate funding requests. Grant makers indicate that **many** impassioned and heartfelt applications—that may otherwise be considered—are often late, unrealistic, vague, unfocused and incomplete, and simply don't make the cut.

Grant makers then ask, legitimately, if the proposal process is in this shape—how will the actual services be delivered and the organization managed? Re-submitting proposals back to Grant seekers, requesting needed information, takes Grant maker time (remembering that 80% have no staff) and ultimately delays your final funding decisions…time that is critical to both the Grant seeker and Grant maker.

When processing hundreds of competing applications with limited or no staff, incomplete applications are put to the side in the pile called "didn't take the time to read the application and follow directions!" **Simple solution:** After all your hard work—don't give the grant maker a reason **not** to consider your worthy, impassioned and heartfelt application for needed services…**your proposal deserves a fair hearing!**

From the Grant maker's perspective, proposals that are incomplete, disorganized, and lack all required elements, such as copy of your actual IRS 501(c)(3) determination letter; tend to suggest that you have really not done your homework. Bottom line: Take the time—invest the time—(make the time!) to get it right. It's really worth it! **A clear and complete application reflects significantly on your capacity and ability to cost effectively utilizes, apply and manage the funding that your organization may receive.**

Important: Your prospect research, community needs assessment, building strategic alliances and partnerships, completing your 501(c)(3) non-profit status, writing proposals and getting funded—can take a year or more depending on federal, state and foundation funding cycles. **You should normally plan on _at least_—6 to 12 months lead-time from the date you are ready to start writing the grant.**

In establishing your initial **brief verbal or written contact with a prospective funder** and building your relationship, in which you have described the project and the grant maker has expressed interest in exploring it further; most Grant makers are more than willing to help and to respond to <u>basic</u> questions.

If you need help—please be sure to ask for the Grant maker's funding guidelines and application, <u>before</u> you submit a full proposal! "Would a project, as described in this one page introductory letter/or this phone call, (1) meet your funding criteria, (2) be something you would be willing to explore further and (3) be appropriate for us to pursue with you at this time?…may be able to be answered. However… "Am I going to be funded?" Is not a question usually answered?

Continue learning and perfecting your grant writing skills and you will begin to realize the unlimited funding potentials your project(s) may receive.

501 (C) (3)
NONPROFIT STATUS

DON'T JUST PURSUE A CAREER—PURSUE YOUR PURPOSE.

"To everything there is a season, and a time to every purpose under the heaven"

(Ecclesiastes 3:1)

501(C) (3) NONPROFIT INCORPORATION

Much of the following information has been made possible from the Internal Revenue Service.

In order for your organization to be classified tax-exempt as an organization described in 501(c)(3) of the Code, an organization must be organized and operated exclusively for one or more of the purposes set forth in 501(c)(3) and none of the earnings of the organization may inure to any private shareholder or individual. In addition, it may not attempt to influence legislation as a substantial part of its activities and it may not participate at all in campaign activity for or against political candidates.

The organizations described in 501(c) (3) are commonly referred to under the general heading of "charitable organizations." Organizations described in 501(c) (3), other than testing for public safety organizations, are eligible to receive tax-deductible contributions in accordance with Publication 170.

The exempt purposes set forth in 501(c)(3) are charitable, religious, educational, scientific, literary, testing for public safety, fostering national or international amateur sports competition, and the prevention of cruelty to children or animals. The term charitable is used in its generally accepted legal sense and includes relief of the poor, the distressed, or the underprivileged; advancement of religion; advancement of education or science; erection or maintenance of public buildings, monuments, or works; lessening the burdens of government; lessening of neighborhood tensions; elimination of prejudice and discrimination; defense of human and civil rights secured by law; and combating community deterioration and juvenile delinquency.

To be organized exclusively for a charitable purpose, the organization must be a corporation, community chest, fund, or foundation. A charitable trust is a fund or foundation and will qualify. However, an individual or a partnership will not qualify. The articles of organization must limit the organization's purposes to one or more of the exempt purposes set forth in 501(c)(3) and must not expressly empower it to engage, other than as an insubstantial part of its activities, in activities that are not in furtherance of one or more of those purposes. This requirement may be met if the purposes stated in the articles of organization are limited in some way by reference to 501(c) (3). In addition, assets of an organization must be permanently dedicated to an exempt purpose. This means that should an organization dissolve, its assets must be distributed for an exempt purpose described in this chapter, or to the federal government or to a state or local government for a public purpose. To establish that an organization's assets will be permanently dedicated to an exempt purpose, the articles of organization should contain a provision insuring their distribution for an exempt purpose in the event of dissolution. Although reliance may be placed upon state law to establish permanent dedication of assets for exempt purposes, the IRS can process an organization's application more rapidly if its articles of organization include a provision insuring permanent dedication of assets for exempt purposes. For examples of provisions that meet these requirements, read Publication 557, *Tax-Exempt Status for Your Organization.*

An organization will be regarded as "operated exclusively" for one or more exempt purposes only if it engages primarily in activities which accomplish one or more of the exempt purposes specified in 501(c)(3). An organization will not be so regarded if more than an insubstantial part of its activities is not in furtherance of an exempt purpose. For more information concerning types of charitable organizations and their activities, see Publication 557.

The organization must not be organized or operated for the benefit of private interests, such as the creator or the creator's family, shareholders of the organization, other designated individuals, or persons controlled directly or indirectly by such private interests. No part of the net earnings of a 501(c) (3) organization may inure to the benefit of any private shareholder or individual. A private shareholder or individual is a person having a personal and private interest in the activities of the organization. If the organization engages in an excess benefit transaction with a person having substantial influence over the organization, an excise tax may be imposed on the person and any managers agreeing to the transaction.

A 501(c) (3) organization may not engage in carrying on propaganda, or otherwise attempting, to influence legislation as a substantial part of its activities. Whether an organization has attempted to influence legislation, as a substantial part of its activities is determined based upon all relevant facts and circumstances. However, most 501(c)(3) organizations may use Form 5768, *Election/Revocation of Election by an Eligible Section 501(c)(3) Organization to Make Expenditures to Influence Legislation*, to make an election under 501(h) to be subject to an objectively measured expenditure test with respect to lobbying activities rather than the less precise "substantial activity" test. Electing organizations are subject to tax on lobbying activities that exceed a specified percentage of their exempt function expenditures. For further information regarding lobbying activities by charities, request Publication "Lobbying Issues" from the IRS.

For purposes of 501(c) (3), legislative activities and political activities are two different things, and are subject to two different sets of rules. The latter is an absolute bar. A 501(c) (3) organization may not participate in, or intervene in (including the publishing or distributing of statements), any political campaign on behalf of (or in opposition to) any candidate for public office. Whether an organization is engaging in prohibited political campaign activity depends upon all the facts and circumstances in each case. For example, organizations may sponsor debates or forums to educate voters. But if the forum or debate shows a preference for or against a certain candidate, it becomes a prohibited activity. The motivation of an organization is not relevant in determining whether the political campaign prohibition has been violated. Activities that encourage people to vote for or against a particular candidate, even on the basis of non-partisan criteria, violate the political campaign prohibition of 501(c) (3). See the FY-2002 CPE topic entitled Election Year Issues for further information regarding political activities of charities.

IRS PROCESSING

User Fee

The IRS has charged a non-refundable processing fee for exemption applications since 1987. There is currently a two-tier fee schedule. Organizations whose gross receipts have averaged, or will average, not more than $10,000 per year pay $150. Larger organizations pay $500. Some experts feel your application will be handled more promptly if you pay the User Fee with a cashier's check or money order. Others disagree. If you pay with a personal check, watch your bank statements carefully to make sure the IRS does, in fact, cash your check for the User Fee. If they don't, your application may have gotten lost in the mail.

A new IRS Revenue procedure announcing the fees comes out each January; if you are submitting your application late in the year, there may be some benefit to getting it in before January 1st.

Mailing Address

Screening

The Covington, Kentucky office should send you a brief letter (Form letter 5548) acknowledging receipt of the application a few weeks after you mail it. All exemption applications are initially screened in Cincinnati to determine whether they can be closed without further development or correspondence with the organization. The typical organization whose application is closed in this way has most or all of the following characteristics: 1) a complete application, 2) "classic" 501(c) (3) activities (an example might be a PTA), 3) a relatively small budget, 4) no paid employees, and 5) no problem areas, such as transactions with insiders, or political activity.

An application the IRS approves without contacting the organization may take only six to ten weeks, start to finish. One quarter to one third of exemption applications receive such treatment. When the IRS feels that additional development is needed, processing is likely to take much longer (four to six months). Not surprisingly, many applicants are interested in expedited handling. Although the IRS is very reluctant to consider any application out of turn, they will sometimes be persuaded by a letter from an unrelated third party, such as a potential grantor, which explains the need for expedited treatment and mentions a specific deadline. Because exemption applications may travel to different parts of the country depending on the IRS workload, a letter of this kind must accompany the application when it is originally submitted.

It probably wouldn't hurt to write, "Request for Expedited Treatment" at the top in large, bold letters, either.

Inquiry Letter

Two thirds to three fourths of the applications the IRS receives require additional development. At the time of this writing (March, 2000) the Cincinnati Service Center is not yet fully staffed, and IRS employees in offices all over the country are handling this phase of processing. When an inquiry letter (Form letter 1312) is sent, you normally have 21 days to respond. If you need additional time, the agent handling the case will routinely grant an extension of ten days to two weeks. If that will not be enough time, however, the IRS usually prefers to close the case (Form letter 1314). Your file is kept in the immediate work area, and reopened automatically when your additional information comes in.

Caution! If you take more than 90 days to submit the additional information, IRS rules say that they can charge you a new "User Fee."

Final Disposition

Once you have answered all of the IRS agent's questions satisfactorily, a favorable determination letter will be issued. There are two main form letters used for a favorable 501(c) (3) determination—Form letter 1045 for an Advance Ruling, and Form letter 947 for a Definitive Ruling.

Here is a summary of several recent years of statistics on the IRS disposition of exemption applications. These statistics cover applications of all kinds, not just 501(c) (3) applications.

Approvals	71%–76%
Denials	.6%–.8%
"Other"	23%–28%

("Other" includes transfer to National Office, failure to provide additional information when requested, and status granted different from status applied for.)

If the IRS denies your application, they must provide you with a written explanation of the facts, law, and argument upon which their decision is based, as well as an explanation of your appeal rights.

EXEMPTION APPLICATION PACKAGE

<u>Forms</u>

1. Form 1023, Application for Recognition of Exemption Under Section 501(c) (3). Make certain that all applicable parts of the form are completed, including any schedules required for your type of organization. An authorized person must sign the form.

2. Form 8718, User Fee for Exempt Organization Determination Letter Request. Attach your check, made out to the IRS, for the applicable fee. Enter "Form 1023" and, if possible, your organization's EIN, in the memo area of the check.

3. Form 872-C (two copies), if the organization is requesting an "Advance Ruling," signed by an authorized person.

4. Form SS-4, Application for Employer Identification Number. This form is not needed if the organization has already had a federal employer ID number assigned.

5. Form 5768, if the organization has decided to elect to make expenditures to influence legislation under section 501(h) of the Internal Revenue Code.

<u>These materials are required; if they are not included, it may delay processing of your application:</u>

1. A copy of the Articles of Incorporation (if your group is incorporated…otherwise, submit your constitution, articles of association, or other governing document—Bylaws alone are not enough). Articles of Incorporation should have the Secretary of State's stamp in the upper right hand corner of the first page. The IRS usually asks for three signatures on the governing instrument of an unincorporated association.

2. Bylaws. These should be signed and dated.

3. Actual financial data, including income statement(s) and a recent balance sheet, if the organization has had any financial activity.

4. A two-year projected budget, showing both expected sources of income and anticipated expenses. Sometimes the IRS asks for a projected budget even when the applicant can provide a full year of actual financial data.

IRS agents reviewing exemption applications often request the following materials:

1. Printed materials describing the history of the organization, its activities and its plans for the future. This might include brochures, pamphlets, descriptive literature, published materials, etc. If you don't have any, it is a good idea to say so somewhere in the application. If you have some in draft form, go ahead and submit them, if that is all that is available.

2. If the organization publishes a newsletter, sample copies.

3. If the group is a membership organization, any materials prepared for members—membership application forms, promotional materials, sample membership certificates or identification cards, sample copies of member-only publications, etc.

4. If you have received media coverage, copies of newspaper clippings, transcripts of interviews, etc.

5. Any documentation you have regarding grant monies. This might include grant applications, grant contracts, or correspondence between your organization and the grantor organization.

6. If appropriate, a "schedule of events," showing where and when your organization has held informational or other events during the last 12 months. Include approximate attendance.

7. If your organization will have a scholarship or grant program:

    •   A description of how potential applicants will hear about your program

    •   A description of eligibility requirements

    •   A sample (draft will do) of the application form(s) you will require applicants to submit

    •   A description of the selection process, including a description of the selection committee itself, and how the selection committee is selected

    •   Any guidelines prepared for the selection committee's use

- Conditions placed upon grants or scholarships, including any requirements for grade notification, etc. and a description of action that will be taken if the terms of the grant are violated

8. In the absence of the several kinds of printed materials described in items 1, 2, 3 and 4 above, it is sometimes useful to have selected letters from your correspondence files, such as letters between your organization and potential members or board members, letters of appreciation from groups where you have made presentations or otherwise helped out, or perhaps even letters from public officials commenting on your efforts.

9. Any or all of the following:

   - Advertisements

   - Actual samples of items you have for sale

   - Copies of contracts, rental agreements, leases, and loan agreements involving the applicant organization

   - Copies of Federal, State or local legislation, if any, regarding the creation or continued existence of the organization

   - Resumes of board members and/or key employees, if readily available, and/or copies of licenses, certificates, etc.

   - Independent appraisals of assets the organization is renting or purchasing from related parties

10. Anything else you may have which would give the IRS insight into your organization's mission or operations.

WHAT QUESTIONS DOES THE IRS ASK MOST FREQUENTLY?

1. Will any officers, directors, members, or their relatives, receive a salary, reimbursement for expenses, or any other form of payment from your organization? If so, explain fully, and include the recipients' names, their duties and the number of hours each week that they will devote to such duties. State the amount of compensation each will receive and the basis for arriving at the amounts of such payments.

2. Please supply a chronology and complete description of all activities of your organization since the date of incorporation, as well as those activities planned for the next 12 months.

3. Please supply copies of literature regarding your organization including, but not limited to, newsletters, newspaper articles, brochures, pamphlets, solicitations for donations, etc.

4. Will anyone use your facility other than for the purpose of directly carrying out your work? Will any of your directors or employees reside at your facility? If so, explain fully. Is the owner of the facility related to you in any way other than as landlord?

5. Will you engage in any publishing activities of any nature? (Printing, publication or distribution of your own material or that printed or published by others and distributed by you)? If "yes," submit the following: (followed by a detailed list).

6. Will you engage in the sale of merchandise? If "yes," submit the following: (followed by a detailed list).

7. Will you engage in the sale of services? If "yes," submit the following: (followed by a detailed list).

8. Will you engage in lectures, or seminars open to the public or to members? If "yes," submit the following: (followed by a detailed list).

ADVANTAGES AND DISADVANTAGES

501(c) (3) Privileges

- Exemption from Federal Income Tax
- Exemption from F.U.T.A.
- Tax Deductibility for Donors
- Eligible for Government & Foundation Grants
- Eligible for Bulk Mailing Permit
- Some B & O and Property Tax Exemptions
- Gambling Permits
- Credibility

501(c) (3) Responsibilities

- Keep Adequate Records
- File Required Returns
- Provide Donor Substantiation
- Obey Disclosure Laws
- Generate Public Support
- Avoid "Excess Benefit"
- Shun Political Activity
- Limit Legislative Activity
- Limit Unrelated Business Activity

The chart below summarizes various kinds of tax treatment for nonprofit and for profit organizations for comparison purposes.

Type of Tax	For-Profit	Non-Profit
Income Tax	Sole proprietor files Form 1040, Schedule C, and pays income tax on net profit. Corporation files form 1120, and pays income tax on net profit; employees file Form 1040 and pay income tax on salaries received	501(c)(3) non-profit files Form 990 or 990-EZ, and pays income tax only on net profit from unrelated activities; employees of the non-profit file Form 1040 and pay income tax on salaries received
Payroll Taxes	Sole proprietorship or corporation files quarterly 941's and annual 940, W-2's and W-3	Nonprofit files quarterly 941's and annual W-2's/W-3, but 501(c)(3) organizations don't pay FUTA tax (Form 940)
Washington B & O Tax: Exempt Purpose Income	Income received by an individual or a for-profit is taxable for B & O tax purposes, even when related to charitable or educational activities	Some income from charitable or educational activities is exempt, while other income may be taxable; there is no blanket rule
Washington B & O Tax: Fundraising activities	Individuals and for profit organizations do not enjoy an exemption for fundraising income	Fundraising activities that meet specific criteria are exempt (examples—rummage sales, fundraising meals, concession sales, auctions)
Property Tax (WA)	Property owned by an individual or a for-profit entity is generally not eligible for property tax exemption	The use of the property determines exemption (examples of uses eligible for exemption—schools, churches, hospitals, nursing homes, museums)
Sales Tax: Sales Income (WA)	Individuals and for profits must collect sales tax on items sold	Some non-profit organization sales can be exempt from sales tax
Sales or Use Tax: Purchases (WA)	Individuals and for profits must pay sales or use tax on purchases	Non-profit organizations must pay sales or use tax on purchases, with very few exceptions
Charitable Contributions	Grantors and contributors are not able to take a charitable contribution deduction for cash or goods donated to an individual or to a for-profit organization	Grantors and contributors are permitted to take a charitable contribution deduction for cash or goods donated to a 501(c)(3) organization

STRATEGIC PLANNING

START WITH REALISTIC, ACHIEVABLE GOALS.

"Commit to the Lord whatever you do,

and your plans will succeed"

(Proverbs 16:3)

STRATEGIC PLANNING & PARTNERSHIPS

This chapter is intended to assist your organization through a full-fledge strategic planning process. The following information will assist your organization in developing an effective strategic plan that will take your organization through the next 1-5 program years. The **XYZ Organization** is a dummy organization referenced throughout the document to assist you *for example purposes only*. If your organization hires a Grant Consultant, some of their responsibilities are outlined below.

ACHIEVING EXCELLENCE

XYZ Organization Strategic Plan

2004–2006

<u>Mission</u>

XYZ Organization's mission is to strengthen and support the ability of nonprofit organizations to serve the Hispanic community, and to enhance public understanding of, confidence in, and support for the nonprofit sector.

<u>Our Vision…</u>

XYZ Organization is a strong and effective countywide association that:

- reflects the Community's sectors richness and diversity,

- provides leadership on issues affecting the sector's current status and future potential,

- sets standards and promotes excellence and accountability in governance and management,

- supports and serves as a resource for nonprofit organizations, boards and staff members,

- builds partnerships with the government, business and philanthropic sectors, and is a reliable source for information about the State's nonprofit sector.

GOALS & STRATEGIES

I. A STATE-WIDE & SECTOR-WIDE ASSOCIATION

XYZ Organization will be an inclusive statewide and sector-wide association. Building on the success of the first years of operation, **XYZ Organization** will continue to grow and expand, recruiting members from every region of the state that reflect the richness and diversity of the state's nonprofit sector. **XYZ Organization** will provide the same level, value and quality of representation, programs and services throughout the state.

Example Strategies

- Develop a local office in Timbuktu County with satellite offices in Area 8.

- Target membership recruitment and expand programs and services into Hargrove counties, the Eastern Shore and Western sectors.

- Establish regional advisory councils to expand opportunities for local nonprofit executives and volunteers to participate in the leadership of the association.

- Refine the association's marketing efforts to more clearly reflect appreciation of the diversity of needs and wants of organizations, regionally, by sub-sector, and by size.

- Revise and expand the committee structure to provide new opportunities for members to participate in determining programs and services to be provided by the association.

- Maintain an involved board representing the diversity of the nonprofit sector, statewide.

II. A LEADER ON ISSUES AFFECTING THE FUTURE OF THE NONPROFIT SECTOR

XYZ Organization will be a leader on issues affecting the current status and future potential of Area 8.

XYZ Organization will continue to be an effective advocate for the Area 8 sector, identifying key strategic issues facing the sector and formulating appropriate solutions. It will promote public policies that are conducive to a healthy and successful nonprofit sector and encourage greater recognition and support for the sector among business, government, and community leaders and the general public. **XYZ Organization** will also provide a voice for the nonprofit sector on important community issues, and will work to assure that the interests of the nonprofit sector and the people nonprofits serve are represented in the public policy debate.

Strategies

- Develop and implement program initiatives to identify and address critical issues affecting the nonprofit sector, including a multi-year public policy agenda.

- Marshal existing research and information, and conduct or encourage others to conduct research, on the state's nonprofit sector with an emphasis on the impact nonprofits have on the quality of life and economic health of the state.

- Use research and information to educate the public about the importance of the nonprofit sector.

- Pursue government funding support to strengthen the infrastructure for nonprofits.

- Continue to promote and support nonprofit sector participation in public policy by providing timely, credible and accessible research and analysis on policy issues affecting important community programs and services

- Strengthen the role of nonprofit organizations as a vehicle for civic involvement by: (a) safeguarding the rights of nonprofits to engage in advocacy, and (b) assisting nonprofit board, staff, and volunteers to attain the knowledge and develop the skills needed to effectively participate in public debate.

- Effectively communicate the interests and needs of nonprofit sector to business, funders, government, the media and the public.

III. A RESOURCE AND SUPPORT FOR BOARDS AND STAFF

As an expert resource for information and assistance on all aspects of nonprofit management, the consultant will help Board Members, Advisory and Volunteer Counsels to compete in an increasingly competitive funding environment.

The Consultant will provide timely, courteous and helpful assistance to **XYZ Organization** their board members and staff on issues affecting the success of their organizations. The Consultant will create opportunities for member organizations to distinguish themselves based on the impact of their work, the quality of their governance, and their commitment to accountability. It will further help members to enhance the skills they need to promote their accomplishments.

Strategies

- Expand the use of new and existing information technologies to improve access to programs and services.

- Refine training and technical assistance programs to allow for more intensive, and or higher level programs and services, tailored to the needs and circumstances of member organizations and to the different levels of expertise of staff and board members.

- Promote and facilitate partnerships and collaboration within the non-profit sector through management innovations, including mergers and joint ventures, and other formal and informal methods.

- Expand training and other services relating to Boards of Directors and individual board members, including: board training, board recruitment and matching, board orientation.

- Continue to facilitate sharing of information and expertise among member organizations.

- Review, upgrade and, where appropriate, expand cooperative buying programs to address the needs of members of different sizes and types.

IV. A STANDARD SETTER, PROMOTING EXCELLENCE AND ACCOUNTABILITY

The Consultant will assist **XYZ Organization** in setting standards and promote effective and accountable governance and management.

The Consultant will aggressively promote the Standards for Excellence to non-profits, funders on behalf of **XYZ Organization**, and the general public as a model for well managed and responsibly governed organizations. It will use the standards to educate the public about the qualities and characteristics of non-profit organizations and to enhance the public's trust in the nonprofit sector.

Strategies

- Provide the educational resources and support necessary to enable organizations to implement the Standards.

- Model the best practices in nonprofit governance and management by implementing the Standards at **XYZ Organization.**

- Provide a voluntary, peer-review certification program to enable nonprofits to demonstrate their adherence to the Standards.

- Provide information about individual nonprofit organizations to donors and prospective donors.

V.   DEVELOPING PARTNERSHIPS AND COLLABORATION

The Consultant will assist **XYZ Organization** in building partnerships that will work collaboratively with the organization, government, business and philanthropic sectors to strengthen communities and improve the quality of life in the Community Area __ region.

The Consultant will work collaboratively with other nonprofit infrastructure support organizations to strengthen **XYZ Organization's** chances of receiving funding. It will build partnerships between a strong nonprofit sector and the government, business and philanthropic sectors to define and promote the best interests of the State of Oregon.

Strategies

- Develop and maintain partnerships with leaders and organizations in the governmental, business and philanthropic sectors.

- Encourage the business and philanthropic communities to invest in the infrastructure of the nonprofit sector.

- Develop one or more advisory boards (e.g. corporate and/or government advisory boards) or community coalition groups.

- Involve other nonprofit sector infrastructure support organizations in activities of the association, and participate in activities of those organizations, where possible and mutually beneficial.

VI. A VALUED COMMUNITY INSTITUTION

XYZ Organization will be a valued and stable community institution, with the board, staff and financial resources needed to expertly serve the needs of the Community Area sector.

XYZ Organization will have a strong organizational infrastructure, with an effective board of directors, a highly skilled, professional staff, up-to-date information technology and adequate support staff. It will have an appropriate physical environment and administrative services to adequately support the provision of high-quality professional services to member organizations and to improve operational efficiency and effectiveness.

Strategies

- Implementing a foundation, government and corporate sustaining support campaign to increase and diversify funding for core programs and services.

- Maintain member dues and program fees as a source of revenue for core program operations.

- Increase level of investment in internal systems and structures, including information technology, facilities, support staff, and personnel benefits and practices.

- Expand the use of information technology, both internally and across all program areas.

- Provide an appropriate senior management structure, which may include an Associate Director and Development/Marketing Director.

- Develop and implement customer service standards to guide **XYZ Organization** staff in serving our members.

- Continue and expand program evaluation efforts to assure relevance and value of association programs and services.

FUNDING SEARCH STRATEGIES

IDENTIFY YOUR MOTIVATION FOR FUNDING.

"In his heart a man plans his course,

but the Lord determines his steps"

(Proverbs 16:9)

SAMPLE FUNDING SEARCH

SEARCH STRATEGIES

The competition for grant monies is fierce, especially so at state, federal, and foundation levels. So, whenever possible, take advantage of funds and donations' at the local level. You may need to use funds and donations from several sources.

Successful mini grant writers usually investigate sources in the following order and ask the following kinds of questions.

1. Building or campus level. Are funds available at the building or campus level? Would the PTA/PTO or other group be willing to provide funds? Are fundraising activities a possible source of revenue? Are students or parents of students able to help persuade or influence local business to donate equipment, materials, or information?

2. District level. Does the district set aside a portion of general funds for projects of this type? Are categorical funds, such as Chapter 1, Chapter 2, and so forth, available for projects of this type? Does the district staff a Grants Department and/or a grant writer who may be able to help secure funds? Does the district have general obligation bond funds, which may be used for projects of this type? Would vendors who regularly provide goods and services to the district be willing to donate equipment, software, materials, etc.? Would the district be willing to consider a partnership with a local college or university, or school district? Would your project have access to equipment, materials, trained staff, and other resources appropriate to your project?

3. Community level. Are there community service organizations whose missions and goals are similar to the objectives of this project? What businesses may be willing to donate equipment and materials to the project? Are volunteers available to donate time and effort to meeting the goals of the project? Does the community receive redevelopment monies for urban or rural renewal? If your organization is within the renewal area, it may be eligible for a portion of the funds. And, your project might be the recipient of some of those funds. Are real estate developers building residential areas within your vicinity? They may be willing to donate to your project, especially if their buyers or their buyers' families might attend your institution.

4. State level. Does your state have a statewide educational improvement program (SIP)? Does your project fit within the guidelines of the SIP? Do state

agencies donate surplus or used equipment and materials? Or, offer equipment at greatly reduced prices to schools and colleges? Do specific states agencies have grant monies available? Consulting services? Technical training? Technical information?

5. Federal level. Under the federal plan for support of social services including education, which programs may be sources of funds for your project? What are their requirements and guidelines? What are the deadlines?

6. Foundation level. Which foundations have missions and goals similar to those of your project? What kinds of projects have they funded in the past? What are the chances they are likely to fund a project like yours?

SAMPLE FUNDING SEARCH
THE ROBERT WOODS JOHNSON FOUNDATION

The Robert Woods Johnson Foundation is offering start-up grants, most for $35,000 each, and technical assistance to help communities organize new Faith in Action coalitions. Over time, the Foundation is seeking to expand the existing Faith in Action network by adding up to 2,000 new coalitions for volunteer care giving that will serve people of all ages and faiths with long-term health problems.

Grants are made to coalitions established by faith congregations (including churches, temples, synagogues, mosques, and other groups with religious missions), as well as by other volunteer organizations or social or health service provider agencies that can demonstrate the participation of faith denominations in the proposed program. Applications are welcome from those who wish to create a new coalition, as well as from existing interfaith coalitions that wish to develop a Faith In Action program.

Applicant organizations must be tax-exempt under Section 501(c)(3) of the Internal Revenue Code and not classified as a private foundation under Section 509(a).

In addition, coalitions:

➢   Serve a geographic area with a population of at least 20,000. Under special circumstances, exceptions may be made to fund coalitions serving a smaller population.

➢   Recruit volunteers from all walks of life.

➢   Organize and train volunteers to provide supportive services to homebound individuals who are frail and elderly or affected by long-term health problems. Supportive services include providing transportation to doctor's appointments, shopping for groceries, cooking meals, doing light housework, running errands, or simply phoning or visiting those who are homebound and lonely because of a long-term health problem. Volunteers may provide relied for those who care for a homebound family member.

THE TELL FOUNDATION

Purpose & Activities: Giving primarily for Christian education.

Fields of Interest: Christian agencies & churches; Elementary/secondary education; Religion; Theological school/education.

Types of support: Building/renovation, equipment, general/operating support; matching/challenging support; program development; scholarship funds.

Limitations: No grants to individuals.   **Deadline:** October 15th

Board meeting date(s): November 18th   **Award amounts:** up to $30,000

NOFA SUMMARY

1. INVITING APPLICATIONS FOR THE RURAL COMMUNITY DEVELOPMENT INITIATIVE (RCDI)

Note: This summary may omit important details. Please consult the Federal Register for complete information. (See below.) This Notice announces the availability of $12 million of grant funds for the RCDI program through the Rural Housing Service (RHS), herein referred to as the Agency, USDA. Applicants must provide matching funds in an amount at least equal to the Federal grant. These grants will be made to qualified intermediary organizations that will provide financial and technical assistance to recipients to develop their capacity and ability to undertake projects related to housing, community facilities, or community and economic development. This Notice lists the information needed to submit an application for these funds.

Agency: USDA

Deadline: 02-Jul-04

Total Funds Available: 12,000,000

Maximum Grant Amount: $50,000 and $1,000,000

Eligible Applicants: 1. The recipient and beneficiary, but not the intermediary, must be located in an eligible rural area. The applicable Rural Development State Office can assist in determining the eligibility of an area. A listing of Rural Development State Offices is included in this Notice. 2. The name and location of recipients must be included in the grant application. 3. The recipients must be nonprofit organizations, low-income rural communities, or federally recognized tribes based on the RCDI definitions of these groups.

Federal Register: DOCID:fr03ap02-37, published 03-Apr-02

For more information, contact: Beth Jones. **Phone:** (202) 720-1498

2. Applications Invited for 2003 HOPE Awards to Promote Minority Homeownership

Deadline: December 2, 2004

The HOPE ("Home Ownership Participation for Everyone") Awards is an industry awards program created by a partnership of real estate associations to honor organizations and individuals who are making outstanding contributions to the promotion of minority homeownership.

Award categories include homeownership education, finance, and project of the year, real estate brokerage, public policy, media coverage, and leadership. Award winners will be chosen by a panel of distinguished judges based on the impact of their work, use of innovative ideas, and acceptance by the minority community, focus on minority homeownership, and focus on affordability.

Each of the award winners will receive a $10,000 honorarium. Winners will also discuss their work and share their experiences with housing policy makers at a symposium at the National Press Club.

Information about the program and application forms is available at the HOPE Awards Web site.

RFP Link: http://www.hopeawards.org/

Center for Health Care Strategies Offers Grants for Oral Health Access

Deadline: June 21, 2004

The Center for Health Care Strategies (CHCS) is accepting applications for up to seven, State Action for Oral Health Access grants of up to $1 million for innovative programs designed to improve access to oral health services.

With funding from the Robert Wood Johnson Foundation, the program will support state-based model demonstration projects, including local system pilots, to test innovative and comprehensive approaches to expanding access to low-income, minority, and disabled populations served through Medicaid, SCHIP, and the public health system. Applicants must be the health, social services, or education agency within a state that is best positioned to execute the demonstration project and is designated as such by the governor. The agency must also show collaboration among key constituencies in the oral health delivery system and have demonstrated experience in improving access to oral health services for underserved populations.

Help Us Help Foundation Offers Tech Grants to Schools and Youth Organizations

Deadline: August 31, 2004; February 28, 2004;

With support from the Oracle Corporation, the nonprofit Help Us Help Foundation assists K-12 public schools and youth organizations in economically challenged communities to obtain information technology tools.

Grants of computer equipment and software are available to schools and youth organizations that provide educational programs in low-income communities. The program will donate new Internet appliances and laser printers as well as all the ancillary equipment necessary to connect the devices, including network hubs, cables, and electrical surge protectors. RFP Link: http://www.helpushelp.org/

Verizon Foundation to Support Community Technology

Deadline: July 12, 2004

The Verizon Foundation, the philanthropic arm of Verizon Communications, is seeking grant applications from nonprofit and educational organizations for community technology development projects.

To qualify for funding, applicants must be a nonprofit organization with a valid 501(c)(3) Internal Revenue Service tax ID. Educational institutions must have a current National Center for Education Statistics for school and district registration. The Verizon Foundation will give strong preference to projects that benefit communities served by Verizon's local phone (non-wireless) companies; emphasize the innovative use of technology in solving problems; assist nonprofit organizations in serving diverse racial and ethnic communities, persons with disabilities, and other underserved groups; and demonstrate collaboration and help improve organizational efficiency.

See the foundation's Web site for complete program guidelines. (Community technology development proposals and other funding requests are accepted only through the Web site.)

National 4-H Council Offers Cooperative Business Plan Awards for Youth

Deadline: July 3, 2004 (extended)

The National 4-H Council, with support from the Rural Business Cooperative Service of the U.S. Department of Agriculture, has announced the availability of five $2,000 awards for the design of a business plan for a cooperative.

The goal of the project is to have youth, in partnership with an adult, write a business plan for a community cooperative. Awardees will not be required to implement the plan; instead, the awards are meant to encourage youth to research cooperatives and learn how to write a business plan for a hypothetical cooperative in the community. The project is not limited to a specific type of cooperative and welcomes plans for agricultural, dairy, housing, utility, health, and other types of cooperatives.

Decisions on awards will be based on how well the business plan includes and addresses the appropriate elements for a business plan, with specific reference to cooperative business elements.

Angel Awards to Honor Children for Community Service

Deadline: June 22, 2004

Georgia-Pacific, maker of Angel Soft bath tissue, is providing support for the third annual Angels in Action Awards Program. The program is designed to reward children and youth who perform exemplary acts of service to benefit a community, charity, or cause.

Ten "Angels" between the ages of 8 and 15 (as of June 22, 2002) will be selected to receive the $5,000 awards. Legal residents of the 50 United States and the District of Columbia and Puerto Rico 18 years or older may submit nominations. Entries will be judged on the nominee's dedication to his or her community, charity, or cause. Nominees must be U.S. residents.

ROBERT WOOD JOHNSON FOUNDATION

Funding Priorities: Aging services; **child development**; civil liberties; disabled; **family services**; **health care** and organizations; **homeless**; general hospitals; medical school; mental health; **minorities**; and **voluntarism promotion**. No set deadline.

Contact Person: Richard J. Toth, Director, Office of Proposal Management

Telephone: (609) 452-8701 or (609) 627-5851   Award **Amount:** $50,000+

CONSULTANT/CONTRACTUAL AGREEMENTS

This funding agency will allow your organization to recapture funds for contractual services.

Consultant: The need for each consultant must be outlined in detail. A work plan for each, including the tasks to be accomplished, should be provided. Fees paid by the Foundation are up to $500/day for a full day of work. For example:

Consultant costs are budgeted at $6,000/year for the participation of Dr. Smith. He will provide expertise in the field of hospital malpractice and serve as our liaison to hospital risk managers and insurers. He will participate in project meetings, refinement and fielding of the questionnaire, review of research methods and draft papers, and work with underwriters and other companies to implement risk-adjusted premiums, as appropriate. The $6,000 estimate is based on twelve days/year at $500/day.

Contractual Agreement(s): For each proposed contract for which you request Robert Wood Johnson Foundation support, you should provide an explanatory paragraph that describes in detail the services to be provided. If possible, you should also provide a separate line-item budget and budget narrative. If the specifics of the contract are not available during budget development, you will need to submit a fact sheet (or a copy of the actual contract) once you have identified the contractor. The fact sheet (or actual contract) should outline the following: * contractor, * dates, * dollars, * tasks/deliverables. The Foundation should not be listed as a party to the contract. The grantee maintains fiscal responsibility for its contracts, which includes reporting expenses associated with the contract to the Foundation. We recommend that you consider including right to audit provisions and record retention expectations when negotiating contracts.

INDIRECT COSTS: Indirect costs may be calculated up to 9 percent on budget categories. However, if **Consultant/Contractual Agreements** (category IV) represents a significant portion of your budget, we reserve the right to negotiate the amount of indirect costs allowed for this category. This line item is intended to cover grant-related costs that are not easily identified but are necessary to conduct the grant, i.e., reporting costs, payroll processing, utilities, space costs, etc. Prorated leased space costs should be identified under the line item **Leased Space** under

OTHER DIRECT COSTS (category II). See Budget Detail Summary in the Appendices section of this book.

Your local government provides grants to community organizations in a variety of areas. The following information briefly describes grant programs administered by the city.

Programs Support:

Arts-In-Education Grants—Matching grants for schools and community organizations to fund artist fees and materials/supplies for arts education projects serving the youth of your city.

Neighborhood Block Watch—Grants up to $10,000 are available to community organizations and Block Watch groups for projects that fight crime and improve the safety and quality of life in neighborhoods.

Consolidated Plan—under the city's consolidated plan with U.S. Housing and Urban Development, a variety of grants and contracts are available to community organizations to provide social services including shelter and medical/dental services to homeless adults and children, housing, neighborhood revitalization and economic development activities. Several city departments administer grants and contracts. Award Amount: $500,000+

Job Training Partnership Act Funds—A variety of employment and training services are funded through a request for proposal process. Services may be provided to youth, adults and displace workers.

HOME INVESTMENT PARTNERSHIP PROGRAM

The Home Investment Partnership Program provides Federal Home funds to the city and other agencies to increase the availability of affordable housing for lower income renters and homeowners. The programs to be funded are Acquisition/Rehabilitation of Rental Housing and First-Time Home Buyers.

Assistance is provided to nonprofit organizations that provide low- and moderate-income housing as well as improve neighborhoods for families and individuals. Services range from assistance in applying for various grants that produce housing to providing matching funds to acquire and rehabilitate housing properties.

Award Amounts: $50,000 to $500,000.

Why do congregations participate in Faith in Action coalitions?

Many faith congregations are already reaching out to people in the community who are in need of assistance from their local churches. However, Faith in Action coalitions can strengthen the efforts of the local assemblies by providing the following:

- ✍ Ongoing assistance in organizing outreach services to those who are homebound.

- ✍ Training for volunteers who visit, transport, and assist those in the home.

- ✍ Assist in locating homebound person(s) who have lost touch within their community.

- ✍ Provide training to the leaders in their congregation who provide oversight for their Outreach Ministry.

GRANT PROPOSAL

DON'T SOW ALL YOUR SEED IN ONE FIELD.

"Sow your seed in the morning, and at evening let not your hands be idle,

for you do not know which will succeed..."

(Ecclesiastes 11:6)

GRANT PROPOSAL FORMAT

Pre-proposal Contact

Grant Application Cover Sheet

Proposal summary

Introduction

Needs assessment

Program goals & objectives

Methods

Program Budget including funds requested and other funding (secured or anticipated)

Evaluations

Appendices (as applicable)

- ✍ IRS statement 501c3 tax exempt status
- ✍ List of board of directors (include addresses and positions)
- ✍ Annual report (990)
- ✍ Most recent audit
- ✍ Evidence of community support (letters of support from clients, constituents, funders)
- ✍ Collateral pieces (brochures, photos, news clippings, etc.)

These templates are available on the latest Grant making Companion Diskette or CD. To obtain these materials, refer to the order page in the back of this book.

NOTE: If the funding source prefers a different outline or format or requests additional information, do as the source directs.

THE PRE-PROPOSAL CONTACT

The purposes of a pre-proposal contact are to determine:

- …if the source's mission and goals are a good match with your project goals;

- …if the source is accepting requests for funding;

- …what kinds of projects are likely to be funded;

- …what guidelines and requirements are;

- …what amount of money or what type of donation is appropriate;

- …what you can do to prepare a successful proposal;

- …what the preferences and biases of the source's proposal reviewers are.

GETTING STARTED

The following timeline is based a three-month estimate. Putting a winning proposal together may seem overwhelming at the start. But, as in doing any complex tasks, proceed step by step. Follow these steps.

1. Identify and document a need for your project. Define the need in terms of the people you serve.

2. Brainstorm with those who may be affected by your project for these reasons:

   - Most needs exist within a social context that means that the viewpoints of those involved are important;

   - If you ask for and listen to others' opinions and ideas, they are more likely to cooperate and support your program, especially if they see some of their ideas incorporated and some of their needs met;

   - Others may offer some great ideas to you.

3. Find out if anyone else in your area or region is planning or doing a similar project. If so, explore the possibility of collaborating. If not, proceed on your own.

4. Form a small advisory group from among those who will be affected by your project. Invite each person to participate and to assist you by giving feedback on your plan and your written proposal, and becoming part of a support group.

5. Develop a timeline. A timeline lets you and others know what must be completed and when. Also, the timeline shows you what you have accomplished and gives important information especially when you are feeling overwhelmed.

6. Develop your plan. Discuss it with a small group—two or three others—and refine it.

7. Perform a funding search for agencies that give grant monies for the program you are focusing on. Focus on identifying a source whose funding goals mesh closely with your project goals.

8. Contact the potential funding source for information and guidelines.

9. Refine your plan so that it fits exactly with the goals and guidelines of the funding source.

10. Share your plan with the advisory group in a formal meeting. Keep a list of those present and record minutes of the meeting. Seek approval and support for your plan.

11. Write the formal grant proposal.

12. Ask two or three others to read your proposal, edit and make suggestions as needed.

13. Revise and polish the proposal as necessary; prepare the finished proposal. Make the required number of copies. Remember to keep at least one copy for yourself.

14. Submit the proposal on or before the deadline. Funding sources adhere to their deadlines. *If you miss a deadline, you're out of business and all of your hard work would have been done for nothing!*

GRANT APPLICATION COVER SHEET

Date of Application:

Legal Name of Organization Applying:

Year Founded: **Current Operating Budget: $**

Contact Person Name & Title:

Address:

City/State/Zip:

Phone Number: **Fax Number:**

Email Address:

Purpose of Grant: (1—2 sentences)

Summary of Organization's Mission:

Project Timeline:

Amount Requested: $ **Total Project Cost: $**

Geographic Area Served:

PROGRAM SUMMARY

The program summary is a bird's eye view or an abstract of what the project is about. It concisely describes your program and should be used for publication purposes. Your program summary should be described in one paragraph. If this is a continuation program be sure to highlight the new services that your organization are providing. The reader should know the who, what, when, where, and why after reading the Program Summary.

Below, you will find an example of a program summary:

> The ABC Organization has been in operation for the past 5 years. Project AEP, a federally funded program is in its' 2nd year of operation. Project AEP provides 20 core lessons in drugs prevention, crime, morals & ethics, gang activity. This curriculum is an provided to the students at Jones Middle School in an intensive learning format in a classroom setting of 893 sixth graders, 2,000 seventh grade students while providing (500) K-8 distance learning courses, and conducting follow-up research on students who have entered into high school levels after taking courses. Since this time 1 private school, 3 public institutions, and 1 elementary school has been added due in large to the Department of Education federal grant funds.

PROBLEM STATEMENT

The purpose of this section is to help you organize your problem statement to grab the reader's attention. It is important during the grant writing process that you make detailed but concise statements when describing the problem, causes, and the long-term impacts. This section of the proposal is critical and it should catch the reader's attention. Here you are proving that you are dealing with a serious and growing problem that must be addressed in order to effectively bring about change. Treat this section as if you were an attorney presenting a case to the jury in a courtroom. You must provide the necessary evidence needed to successfully win your case. This section should confirm without a reasonable doubt that you have a need! Keep in mind that this emotional appeal will catch the reviewers' attention and draw them into your proposal! In other words, they will begin to feel sorry for your organization…and that's a good thing!

I.   NEEDS ASSESSMENT/DEFINING THE PROBLEM

A.   The first purpose of the needs assessment is generally to define the problem and describe what caused the problem.

Ask yourself these questions:

1.   What are the current needs to be addressed in the community in which we are serving?

2.   Who is currently addressing these needs?

3.   What are the gaps in services in order for the participants to get their needs met? (e.g., transportation, childcare, etc.)

4.   How will we assist in filling in the gaps?

5.   Who will benefit from our services?

6.   What are the origins to this problem that we are addressing?

7.   What will happen if nothing is done about this problem or need?

8.   What is already functioning well?

9.   What resources do I already have? (Focus on your strengths here.)

10.   Can I collaborate with already existing organizations to assist in effectiveness? (If applicable)

Remember here that you are building your case. Remember to include statistics, actual stories, etc.

B.   Decide what the problem is.

Ask yourself these questions:

1.   The target population is the recipient of the program or project. This group of individuals is the focal point of the program and will reduce the effects of the problem. Who is the target population (i.e. at-risk students)? Who is the secondary target population (i.e. parents)? Who will be affected by this problem? The actual numbers shows that this project will impact a significant number of people. Who will benefit? Be sure to include as much information about the participants that will be involved in your program as possible.

2. he geographic area is the sphere of people that you are targeting. It is usually a geographic location, community or residential area, or district. Where is the target population located? What area are we addressing? You may distinguish the regional area by zip codes, county, city, or region.

C.   Gather data to prove and determine the extent of your problem or need.

Ask yourself these questions:

1.   What type of data will I need to outline the problem?

2.   What evidence and/or information demonstrate that there is truly a problem or need.

3.   What types of data should I collect to show evidence that there is a problem or need that exists?

Examples:

- **Statistics**

- **Social indicators**

- **Per capita income**

- **Population below poverty**

- **Teenage pregnancy rates**

- **Divorce rates**

- **Crime rates**

- **School dropouts**

- **Juvenile delinquency**

- **Infant mortality and deaths**

- **And the list goes on….**

> **Find evidence that further reinforces what you are trying to convey.**

D.   Find resources where you can acquire data to determine the need.

Ask yourself these questions:

1. Where can I go to find out more information about my problem?

2. Is there an expert who knows about this problem in the community?

3. Is there a "Report of Findings" for my area? Check with the City.

4. What approaches or methods should I use in order to address this need?

E. Use popular sources to acquire data.

1. Chamber of Commerce

2. Local, county, or school district

3. Conduct focus groups to obtain data

4. Interview people in the community

5. Review relevant materials such as newspapers, journals, magazines articles, and books.

Writing the Problem Statement

A. Organization

1. Begin organizing your material and writing the problem statement. Keep in mind that you want to provide your reader with a quick review of the problem.

2. Start off your section with a short, 'concise' sentence that describes your problem in detail.

   ✍ The problem is...

3. This sentence should define the causes for the problem.

   ✍ The causes of the problem are...

4. Tell the reader what will happen, in the long run, if an intervention does not occur (your scare tactic).

   ✍ If no intervention were performed at this time, long-term effects for the residents of this community would be detrimental.

B. Categorize your problem statement by examining the problem from different perspectives. This shows the grant reviewer that you have taken the time to look at the problem from different angles and will further engage the reviewer into your project. This will allow the reviewer to stay focused. You must remember to keep your center of discussion around the problem and use your needs assessment and gathered data to substantiate the need. Some examples include:

- The causes of the problem are…

- Here is a sample: "To what extent is child abduction preventable? Empirical studies are unable to fully address this issue since the measurement of "lost opportunities" for abductors by children who have been empowered with the relevant knowledge, attitudes, and skills eludes quantification. To neglect prevention because this problem does not lend itself to precise measurement and prediction is to invite still more tragedies."

- More examples include:
    a. According to recent surveys dated January 1, 1999…

    b. _____ County is #2 in the State for below poverty.

    c. The rate of (crime, welfare assistance, dropouts, etc.) has (decreased, increased).

    d. By examining the chart below, you will find….

C. Be sure to include descriptive words while you are creating your problem statement. Some words to think of: highest, lowest, high-risk, substandard, inadequate, deficit, severe, disregarded, increased, outbreak, bleak, etc.

D. Additional Hints

- Include statistics in each category that will support your problem statement and its' long term effects.

- Statistics should come from a variety of sources.

- The problem statement will not include program activities.

- You must convince the reader that the problem is an actual problem that is both growing and serious.

- Use real numbers when using statistics, do not spell them out.

- Reference sources that you retrieve your information from.

- Be sure to include a reference page in your Appendix section.

E.   Conclude your problem statement section with both a transitional point that will take the reader to the next section of the proposal and a wrap up statement that will provide an overview of the problem in the community.

   ✍ Example: Our program will decrease the amount of gang activity by 20% in Sunset Ridge neighborhood by offering teenagers…**OR**

   ✍ The problem continues to grow….

F.   Reread your problem statement really well to make sure that the reader understands and is moved by the situation so much so that they want to give your organization the money!

ANTHONY HOLLIS   •   61

EXAMPLE: PROBLEM STATEMENT

NEED FOR PROGRAM

The problem that Sunset Ridge Community is facing is that there are many high-risk families in our community that are illiterate. The effect from illiteracy has caused an increase in the levels of poverty, unemployment, lack of motivation to find jobs or improve their education. Long-term effects without the proper intervention will cause these destitute families to remain in a continued cycle of poverty; live in deplorable conditions, increase gang activity, governmental dependency, and have a generation of children who feel neglected, unwanted, and unloved.

Tahoe County ranks among the highest in the county with both poverty and the lease amount of resources available to individuals in the State of Oregon. The Sunset Ridge Community that is represented in this proposal is often overlooked and discounted and seen by many motorist as a convenient store and gas-stop on the way to the coast. While being plagued by interrelated issues resulting from poverty such as drugs and alcohol, serious health problems, crime, illiteracy, and governmental dependency has caused many families to become trapped in a survival mode which leads to unhealthy lifestyles.

The following statistics illustrate the plight that many families in our community are facing, most of which are African-Americans and Hispanics.

Social Indicator	Tahoe County	Oregon Average	County Ranking (out of 36 Counties)
Illiteracy rate	68%	34%	33rd worst
% Single parents	42%	31%	34th worst
% births to single moms	35%	25%	32nd worst
% families below poverty	31%	21%	35th worst
% failed grades 1-3	38%	26%	25th worst
% without telephone service	22%	10%	29th worst
% children < 2 yrs old without immunizations	59%	—	—
% children not ready for kindergarten	40%	30%	—
% families without transportation	18%	11%	—

Clearly, the statistics show the people of Tahoe County are very distressed and in need of intensive assistance. Critical resources are vital in order to aid the number of families in the area. The Employment Security Commission of Oregon has reported Tahoe County with the highest unemployment rate in the state (18%) in June 1999!

STAFF PERSONNEL

In the proposal you will be asked to give a brief job description of the individuals who will be working in the program. These individuals should have experience with working with the target population you are serving. If no one has experience, training and possible certifications should be conducted as soon as possible. You may include this as a line item in your budget as well as in your budget detail summary page. Hiring professional personnel such as doctors, nurses, etc. may be necessary depending on your project.

✍ Mrs. Cunningham is the Executive Director of ABC Organization Alternate Educational Program (AEP). She has been in alternative education for over 15 years. Xavier McDonald, Program Coordinator of the Computer Learning Lab, and Yolanda Perez, Cliff Parris, Elijah Harris, and Martha Silverstein instructs students with TEA curriculum. Each staff personnel are experienced and have been working in their designated fields for an average 10 years. Each has worked with multi-disciplined, at-risk, and diverse groups of individuals.

Briefly describe how your organization works: What are the responsibilities of the board, staff, volunteers, and, if a membership organization, the members?

How representative are these groups (board, staff, etc.) of the communities with which you work? Please outline general demographics of the organization.

Who will be involved in carrying out the plans outlines in this request? Include a brief paragraph summarizing the qualifications of key individuals involved.

Provide a list of your board of directors with related community and employment affiliations.

Organizational charts showing decision-making structure.

PROGRAM DESCRIPTION, GOALS & OBJECTIVES

Program Description outlines in detail your overall program plan. It clearly addresses each portion of the program and its' priority requirements. In your program or project description, you must outline, in a chronological format, your project goals (what you are setting out to achieve) and explain how each of your program activities will assist your organization in achieving these goals. This gives the reader a better understanding of how your organization will impact the need that has been presented in the proposal.

In this section, you are to include a description of the program activities, position descriptions of all personnel that your organization need to be funded by federal, state, or foundation grant monies.

Program Goals are overall goals that you set out to achieve. You direct your program activities towards each goal. Each grant proposal must contain at least one program goal.

- ✍ Reduce substance abuse among teenagers between the ages of 13—15.

- ✍ Involve local middle schools in the project and planning process.

Program objectives are goals that you are hoping to achieve in a systematic approach. They are specific and the results are either measured in a qualitative or quantitative approach. The results are realized through a number of activities that you have strategically planned for in the proposal. The objectives must relate to the problem and they describe who will work on the project, by when and why.

- ✍ The goal of Project AEP is to prevent middle school students between the ages of 12-15 from engaging in gang related activities, substance abuse, and criminal-like behavior at the middle school level. The ABC Organization will achieve this goal though the performance of the efforts of Project AEP.

- ✍ To achieve a reduction of 45% gang activity within the 8th grade level through education, group therapy, and visits to local prisons and correctional institutions.

- ✍ Officers from the local police department, correctional institutions, and detention centers will provide the D.A.R.E. core curriculum during the 2000—2001 school year to approximately 4,000 students. The expected results is by August 2002, there will be an increase of 90 percent or more students who has an increase awareness of gang activity and substance abuse opportunities and ways to avoid these pressures.

METHODS

The methods are specified steps and activities that your program will take in order to reach the stated objectives. While describing the methods you are undertaking, a timeline would be appropriate in this section.

- Students will enroll in an open-entry, open exit-learning situation, which emphasizes computer-based learning, supplemented and extended by learning groups. Students will attend a one-hour course in accordance to their schedules between the hours of 8:00 am—6:00 pm. They will also spend at least 2 hours per week in a cooperative learning group therapy session, 1 hour in the D.A.R.E. program taught by local law enforcement officers, as well as spend one hour per day reading newspaper articles, periodicals, and other appropriate print materials including literature suited for their age group. Each student's progress will be tracked and will automatically be assigned to the appropriate materials needed for learning. Each instructor will review each student's progress daily, facilitate learning groups, and make appropriate recommendations as needed.

By now, your thinking process for this portion of the grant-writing proposal should be as follows:

Need for Project: (State need in terms of what needs to be accomplished.)

Target Group: (Describe those who will be the participants in your program. Be specific to age, gender, race, ethnicity, at-risk, etc.)

Personnel: (Describe who will be involved and what their roles will be. Mention their relevant experience with working with the target population.)

Objectives: (These are the outcomes you want to attain.)

Method: (Describe the activities which will be used to reach those objectives.)

..........AND HERE COMES T-H-E BUDGET

These are the actual costs that will be needed in order for the program to run. In the budget summary detail portion of the grant proposal, you will describe in detail the line items needed for the program and their costs. The budget should accurately reflect the goals and objectives of the program. They should be reasonable and accurate. Do not pad the proposal in hopes that you will receive more funding. Develop a budget and stick to it and remember, the funding agency in which you are requesting funds from has a budget too!

Items to include are as follows:

1. Organization's current annual operating budget.

2. Current project budget (Use NNG format in the Companion Worksheet).

3. List individually other funding sources for this request. Include amounts and whether received, committed, or projected or pending.

4. Most recent completed year's organizational financial statement (expenses, revenue, and balance sheet), audited, if available and/or applicable.

5. A copy of your IRS 501(c)(3) letter. If you do not have a nonprofit status under the IRS, check with the funder to see if they are willing to fund through your fiscal sponsor, or are willing to exercise expenditure responsibility.

3 DZA Reading Series and Math Competency Skill Building Lab Packs (of 10 each) which

include reading and math programs from primer to 10 grade levels...... ....$8,500.00

3 DZA Reading Series and Math Competency Skill Building Lab Packs (of 10 each) which include reading and math programs from primer to 10 grade levels	$8,500.00
10 hours of teacher training workshops for the 5 staff members	$2,400.00
100 new picture/story/DZA books for substance abuse students: approximately $5 each	$750.00
Purchase of workplace attitude, grooming, dress videos: approximately $89.95 each for 6 videos	$539.70
TOTAL	$12,189.70
Other Costs: *(This shows that all avenues of funding have been explored and tapped.) Additional In-kind services will be noted here.*	
10 Hewlett Packard Computers (secured by donation)	$9990.00
5 Hewlett Packard LaserJet 2100M Printers (secured by donation)	$3995.00
TOTAL (secured by donation)	$13,985.00

EVALUATION

Last, but certainly not least, is the evaluation portion that is required by most funding agencies. The evaluation is a key element in the grant application process. An evaluation team should be formed. Each team should be comprised of representatives from the board, community, and participants of the program. The evaluation methodology should contain four quality standards. These standards are feasibility, utility, propriety, and accuracy.

Feasibility standards are used to ensure that the evaluation that is used by the organization or program is diplomatic, realistic, and cost-effective. This is done by using practical procedures and cost-effective measures. Practical procedures refer to how the information is collected. The evaluation portion should be is a manner that is not disruptive to the staff, volunteers, or participants involved in providing the information. The evaluation portion should also be collected in a manner that is cost-effective for the program wherein a significant amount of resources is not expended in order to make this happen.

Utility standards are used to ensure that the evaluation tools that are needed will serve the needs of the intended users. The team will develop measuring tools needed to facilitate responses that track the needs and interests of all that are involved. The team will interpret and report all findings to be published in the organization's annual report. The program agrees that the evaluation will be planned, conducted, reported, and disseminated in a written format to the Board of Directors as well as to the funding agency that is providing grant monies to the organization.

The **proprietary standards** are here to ensure that the evaluation portion of the program is conducted morally, ethically, and with due diligence in regards to all person(s) that are involved in and affected by the program. This part of the evaluation serves as a program monitor. What it says to the funder and to the Board of Directors is that the program is or is not providing the services outlined in the grant application to the program participants. This portion of the evaluation also says that everyone involved in completing the program evaluation piece will not be threatened in any way and that they will be treated with respect.

The **accuracy standards** set by the organization will ensure that the purpose and process of the evaluation will be monitored and described in detailed for anyone who needs access to the evaluation. All paperwork that is submitted will be submitted in an accurate manner with clear and concise detail. Also, the information that is given will be reliable, formatted in a quantitative and qualitative nature, and is valid.

Evaluations should always show what your organization has accomplished in a certain timeframe. They describe which of your objectives that were accomplished and were not accomplished, and to what extent your program was a success.

SUPPORT MATERIAL

Letters of support (up to 3)

Recent organization materials

> Newsletters
> Brochures
> Articles
> Newspaper clippings
> Evaluations
> Reviews (up to 3)

Recent annual report

Organization Letterhead

THE AWARD DECISION

The day that you have been waiting for has finally arrived. The long awaited award decision letter from your funding source finally arrives. You nervously open the letter to see whether or not your proposal will be funded.

Will it or won't it? If the news is good and your grant proposal is funded, treat yourself to a celebration dinner. But keep in mind; the cerebration period will be brief for there is much work that lies ahead.

Generally, the letter of acceptance will explain the next steps, which usually include contacting the source for further information. Follow the directions in the letter promptly and send a thank you letter to the funding agency quickly. You would be surprised at the number of organizations that don't say *THANK YOU!* So dare to be different and give **THANKS!**

If your proposal is not funded, do not be discouraged. Instead, ask for feedback on the proposal. Although reviewers are busy, they are helpful and generally provide written feedback as well as a rating on the different parts of the proposal. You may choose to make changes suggested by the reviewers and resubmit the proposal to the same funding source at a latter date. Or, you may wish to submit your proposal to a different funding source. Either way, do not give up. Many times a proposal is rejected because the mission and goals of the funding source did not mesh closely enough with your project goals, in spite of all your homework. There are other times that a proposal may not be funded because of the amount of funds that the funding agency has to distribute to the large number of applications received.

MANAGING YOUR GRANT FUNDS

Winning a grant is almost a mixed blessing. Not only are you ecstatic that you have been awarded the funds that you were seeking, but reality begins to set in and you realize that now your real work begins! It's time to translate those ideas into action. You will have additional paperwork, meetings to attend, and reports to prepare. Being well organized is the key to successfully managing your grant.

The following suggestions will lead your organization to success.

1. Reread your proposal, especially the objectives, methods, and evaluation plan. Form a clear picture of exactly what you said you would do and when.

2. Prepare a detailed timeline of events, who is responsible, and when the task or event should be complete.

3. Make arrangements for rooms, transportation, supplies, equipment, etc., far in advance. Meet with your administration to enlist cooperation and to ensure that your project does not interfere with regular operations.

4. Organize your correspondence. Keep track of assistance and contributions and acknowledge that help with thank you letters. Keep a copy of all correspondence.

5. Establish a storage place for all grant related matters. A file folder, a separate box or drawer, or a file cabinet should be used exclusively for your grant.

6. Be very meticulous with all of your bookkeeping. You will be accountable for all expenditures. If you need assistant to handle you're bookkeeping needs considering retaining an accountant or bookkeeping consultant.

7. Arrange for publicity for activities and achievements in connection with your grant. Contact the newspaper, TV stations, and others several weeks in advance of the activity to make arrangements for coverage.

8. Evaluate each activity or event as it takes place. Assess the results, collect and retain data, write summary statements of the results. This will make writing the summary report much easier.

9. Take photographs or videos during activities or events. Ask participants to sign release statements giving you the rights to the photos and videos. These give you additional documentation of your activities and are excellent PR materials.

10. When you prepare summary reports, emphasize positive outcomes. Support your statements with data. Draw logical conclusions and make recommendations.

CORPORATE LETTER REQUESTS

PRAY THAT YOUR CORPORATE REQUESTS BE ANSWERED.

"Do not be anxious about anything, but in everything,
by prayer and petition…present your requests to God"

(Philippians 4:6)

CORPORATE LETTER REQUEST FORMAT

The Corporate Letter Request should include the following format. After conducting a formal funding search for Corporations who fund your particular program interest, be sure to go through the following format for requests.

- Date

- Opening Address

- Salutation

- Introductory Paragraph in bulleted format

- Introduce your organization

- State your problem or need (2—3 paragraphs)

- Plead your case filled with traumatic situations

- State how the funding agency can help to solve your problem

- Ask for the money and let the funding agency know what you are going to do with the money

- Ending greeting

- Sign letter

- Postscript (P.S.) including one more emotional sentence

- Enclosures (if applicable)

Senior Citizen Corporate Letter Request

Next you will find an actual corporate letter that was used to receive funding for a senior citizen project conducted in Raleigh, North Carolina. Names have been changed to protect the identity of individuals and the confidentiality of the ministry who received the funding.

SENIOR CITIZEN CORPORATE LETTER REQUEST

January 1, 2004

Contact Name

Position

Funding Source Name

Address

City/State/Zip

Dear Mr./Ms./Mrs. (Last name):

- For Geraldine (use a food and medicine description)

- Transportation is limited in the _____ area of Southeast Raleigh. Mr. Johnson who lives in this area has no means of transportation therefore; he has no transportation to and from the pharmacy to pick up his heart medication.

- Being an elderly citizen in the Southeast Raleigh area, without transportation and care could mean a day in the life without food, the proper medications residents will develop malnutrition, a significant decline in health, which could eventually lead to death.

The (name of the program) is an outreach program for the Better Living Resources community economic development corporation located in Wake County. The program serves the needs of the elderly in the Southeast Raleigh area branching out to cover areas such as (input other neighborhoods you plan to cover).

Since (month/year) our (# of) staff and volunteers have provided food, clothing, and transportation for the elderly to and from the grocery store, the pharmacy and the doctor. These elderly persons have felt abandoned in their homes without the love and support of their family members and without the proper care needed to survive in this society.

Thanks to the (name of the program here), the elderly receive groceries, nutritional meals, and are able to take the physician prescribed medications, but we need your help. Each month a driver picks up seniors such as Mr. Johnson and takes him to the doctor and the pharmacy. Each time Better Living Resources provide services to the elderly we expend $_____.00 per person for a one month period. Thus far this year, our services have exceeded $____.00 in costs. While we are supported through contributions from the members of (organization or religious affiliation), the current year's revenue is only $____.00. Based on our costs per senior citizen, only ____# of persons can benefit 3 months left in the calendar year we only have funds for an additional (timeframe) month. You see we average (#) of seniors per month. The elderly in Southeast Raleigh are begging for our help.

In turn, we humbly plead to your spirit of generosity and compassion. Rather than ask for $25, $50, etc. we are leaving the amount up to you (or you may ask for a certain amount).

Tonight, Ms. Geraldine and Mr. Johnson have eaten a well-balanced, nutritional meal, taken their medicines and are taken care of, but how many other citizens, our mothers and fathers, our grandparents are left out there without meals, without a way to the doctor, without medications, and without an indication of how they will make it physically and mentally for the next day, month, and year.

Please send any contributions to Jane D. Smith, Development Director. Make your checks payable to Better Living Resources.

Thank you in advance for this overwhelming show of support for our seniors.

Warm regards,
Jane D. Smith
Development Director
Enclosures

GRANT WRITING STRATEGIES

HONESTY IS STILL THE BEST POLICY IN GRANT WRITING.

"The integrity of the upright guides them, but the unfaithful are
destroyed by their duplicity"
(Proverbs 11:3)

GRANT WRITING TIPS & STRATEGIES

Fund-raising is not raising money; it is about networking raising friends.

You do not raise money by begging for it; you raise it by selling people on your organization and your programs.

People do not just reach for their checkbooks and give money to an organization; they have to be asked to give.

You don't wait for the "right" moment to ask; you **ASK NOW!**

You don't decide today to raise money and then ask for it tomorrow.

It takes…

- ✍ time,
- ✍ patience, and
- ✍ planning to raise money.

Prospects and donors are not cash crops waiting to be harvested. Treat them as you would your customers in a business setting.

Myths about fund-raising

- ✍ the process is a mystery
- ✍ you need a proven track record to be successful
- ✍ corporations and foundations give most of the money

Three Things You Should Do Before Asking for Money

- ✍ Review Your Mission
- ✍ What Will You Do With the Money?
- ✍ Plan and Plan Some More

ALWAYS SAY THANK YOU TO THOSE WHO HELP YOUR PROGRAM
TO BE A SUCCESS!

Funding Agencies	**Participants**
Volunteers	**Board Members**
Advisory Committees	**Staff Personnel**

How To AVOID PITFALLS

Foresight and careful planning are crucial to the grant writing process. However, other obstacles may occur. The following suggestions should help you avoid the obvious pitfalls in grant writing.

1. Emphasize outcomes and benefits to the target population. Never mind that you are requesting the latest computer system because the voters did not pass the latest technology bond issue at the last election, but rather emphasize the fact that student achievement will be gained through the addition of up-to-date computer technology for the purposes of educational learning.

2. Clearly show how your project fits with the mission and goals of the funding agency. In your cover letter, restate the goals of the funding source as well as your own project goals to reinforce the compatibility.

3. In your statements of need and benefit, convey a sense of urgency and importance. When your personal reviewers read your draft proposal, ask them if that urgency was conveyed. If not, revise the necessary portions to reflect the urgency. The reviewer must be convinced that your proposal, above all the others, **must** be funded.

4. Clearly specify the objectives of your project. The objectives are the outcomes. They must be measurable and the evaluation procedures are clearly stated in the appropriate section of the proposal.

5. Include a well-developed evaluation plan. The evaluation should consider outcomes on several levels including students, parents, community, faculty and staff. Funding sources usually require evaluation reports either during the period of the grant or at the end of the grant. Be sure to accurate report your findings.

6. Write concisely, simple, and directly. Avoid jargon and rat holes. Revise, edit, and revise until the proposal is a polished and professional product.

7. Develop your proposed project with the help of an advisory group. Mention the use of the advisory group in the proposal. This tells the funding source several things: your project has institutional support; it is compatible with the institutional goals and objectives; it has the support of your immediate peers; it represents the thinking of a work group and not the personal preference of an individual.

8. Follow the guidelines and instructions from the funding source to the letter. Be aware of what items and activities are allowable, the deadline data, the assurances and letters of support required, the number of copies that must be submitted, and so forth. If the guidelines state that you are limited to a certain number of pages, then limit your proposal to that number and not one paragraph more.

9. Submit the proposal on or before the deadline. **Late proposals are not accepted**! Make sure that the proposal carries a postmark acceptable to the funding source. Generally, the postmark from the U. S. Postal Service, the certified letter/return request, and postmarks from the private mail carriers (Federal Express, etc.) are acceptable. Also, many funding sources will permit you to hand deliver your proposal. If you are allowed to send your proposal through electronic mail, be sure that you receive a confirmation report that the funding agency has received your proposal.

10. Never lie, deceive, or misuse funds in any way. Funding agencies talk to each other. Your organization's name is at stake and can become ruined if you misrepresent your organization or mislead an agency in any way, thereby jeopardizing future funding. If a mistake is made or you discover that you did not report a finding accurately, simply contact the funding agency right away. Remember, grantors are accountable for funds distributed, just as the grantee is accountable for funds to be used.

FREQUENTLY ASKED QUESTIONS

KEEP A JOURNAL OF BUSINESS IDEAS AND LESSONS LEARNED.

"Then the Lord said to Moses, Write this on a scroll as something to be remembered"

(Exodus 17:14)

FREQUENTLY ASKED QUESTIONS (FAQ)

The following information is not intended to be legal advice and should be used only as a guide for general use only. If you have questions about incorporation, tax-exemption or any of the following information, you should consult an attorney, accountant, or professional consultant.

What is an EIN number and how do I get one?

EIN is the acronym for Employer Identification Number. This Employer Identification Number is assigned to your organization by the Internal Revenue Service employer identification number. See the instructions that accompany SS4 Publication for more information.

What IRS forms do I need in order to form a 501 (c) (3) Nonprofit Corporation?

You will need to file form 1023 for recognition as a tax-exempt **501 (c) (3)** organization. You can download these forms from the www.irs.gov website or obtain them directly from the Internal Revenue Service. Publication 557 contains all the information about nonprofit tax-exemption as well as general information about nonprofit regulations. You should also consider hiring an attorney, accountant or consultant to complete these forms for you, as they can be very complex in nature.

What does 501 (c) (3) mean anyway?

It refers to the section of the IRS code that describes what we typically refer to as nonprofit charitable organizations. There are other types of nonprofits as well.

How long does it take to receive my 501 (c) (3) tax-exemption?

There is no way to predict how long the process will take. Generally speaking, 3-5 months is a good estimate. The process can take longer if the IRS has questions concerning your organization. You must reply promptly in order the IRS to complete your application.

Can my organization accept donations while the application is being processed?

Yes, as long as your organization informs donors that are giving their contributions that their gifts may not be tax deductible if your application is refused.

Can I send my grant proposal application in electronic form?

Many foundations, corporations, and governmental entities are now accepting applications via electronic mail. Although e-mail is available in electronic form for your convenience in completing the application, it is the responsibility of the organization that is applying for funds to verify that the funding agency received their application. However, there are many funding agencies that do not as of yet accept completed applications in electronic form. Follow the instructions for applications provided on the application.

Is the grant deadline the postmark date or day the funding agency receives it?

For the ongoing grant programs, proof of a postmark is sufficient. For applications that respond to an RFA (Request For Application) or RFP (Request For Proposal), applications must be received at the funding agency by close of business on the deadline date.

Can any changes be made after the grant application is mailed?

Every effort should be made to submit a complete, intact application, including letters of support from the onset. Although no promises can be made that changes will be made to your proposal, if you find typos, paging or budget errors and if there are significant changes that will make the difference in your program, contact the program officer responsible for the grant program.

Who decides whether my grant gets funded?

The decision to fund any given grant, in many cases, is made by a panel of experts, which have considerable experience with the granting process for that particular funding agency. Awards are based on scientific merit (as reflected by the priority score), relevance to the funding agency's program mission, and available funds.

What are the steps in the review process and how long does it take?

The review process is set exclusively by the agency that your organization is requesting grant funding from. Completely review the grant application guidelines, which outline the grant review process from the time an application is received until a funding decision is made. If guidelines are not available, contact the funding agency that you are applying to.

What is the numerical priority score?

After discussing an application, members of the review group privately vote a numerical score. The normalized average of the scores constitutes the priority score, which is assigned by the funding agency. Federal scores are given for each section of the request for proposal (rfp).

If I get a good priority score, will my grant be funded?

All grant awards depend on availability of funds, relevance to funding agencies priorities, and the balance of grants in funding agency's grant portfolio.

Will I get a written evaluation of my grant?

Approximately 6-8 weeks after your application is reviewed, you will receive a written evaluation of your application called the Summary Statement

If I don't get funded, can I apply again?

You may submit up to two revisions of your application within 3 years of the original date of submission. The steps for submitting a revised application are described in the funding agency's application.

What happens to my application if I don't get funded?

Most applications are left active for up to two years from the original date of submission, during which time it may be considered for funding.

Should I revise and reapply or start over on a new grant?

It depends on the nature of the specific weaknesses or problems in your proposal. Some "fatal flaws" are fairly straightforward and simple to identify and correct; others are less so. When reviewers assess an amended application, they look to see how shortcomings identified in the summary statement are addressed, but will also review the entire proposal, as a whole, for strengths and weaknesses. Sometimes, fixing one set of problems reveals another set. Thus your priority score could actually go up (worsen) for a revised application.

Do I have to make every change the reviewers suggested?

You don't have to make all the changes suggested by the reviewers, but you should respond to them in your introductory section, and explain your rationale for making or not making recommended changes

Will the funding agency send me a notice if my application is funded?

If your organization has provided an e-mail address, an electronic Notice of Grant Award letter is sent from the funding to the administrative official listed on the face page of your grant application. A courtesy copy of the e-mail is sent to the principal investigator of a successful application. If your organization does not use e-mail, the Notice of Grant Award will be faxed to the administrative official listed on the face page of your application. The funding agency's program officer assigned to the grant may contact the principal investigator to give informal news of an award, but the Notice of Grant Award is the official documentation and will be mailed to the organization.

How do I get access to my grant funds?

Access to grant funds are arranged through the funding agency's Payment Management System. Federal funds are usually deposited in a grantee's bank account. Instructions on how to gain access to grant funds are sent to the administrative official listed on the face page of your grant application.

Why if I don't get the budget I requested?

The funding agency's review committee makes a budget recommendation for each application it reviews. In some cases, that recommendation is to reduce the budget. The staff may also reduce the budget for programmatic reasons or because available funds are not sufficient to provide full funding.

My Notice of Grant Award says the grant is excluded from "expanded authorities"—what does that mean?

For certain types of grants some funding agencies may waive the requirement for its prior approval of certain expenditures and activities. If your grant is excluded from expanded authorities, you must seek prior approval for budget carryover and no-cost extensions.

What if I need more money?

Budget supplements may be allowed, depending on need and the availability of funds. Contact the funding agency's Program Staff that has been assigned to your organization and is responsible for your grant to discuss the availability of a budget supplement.

Who owns the equipment and material purchased with grant funds?

The grantee owns equipment and material purchased with grant funds unless the award specifies something different.

What kinds of reports are required during the grant period?

A progress report is due two months before the end of each year of grant-funded activity

What kinds of final reports are required after the grant ends?

The most requested reports, which are due when, grant funding ends are the Financial Status Report and a Final Project Progress Report. These reports serve as *accountability* and *stewardship purposes only* to assure that the grant funds were used properly. These reports are not used to "snoop" or "spy" on the organization

APPENDICES

SAMPLE
LINE ITEM BUDGET

COUNT THE HIDDEN COSTS.

"Suppose one of you wants to build a tower. will he not first sit down and estimate the cost to see if he has enough money to complete it?"

(Luke 14:28)

SAMPLE LINE ITEM BUDGET

(Institution Name)

Grant Period: (from ___/____/____ to ____/____/___)

Budget Period: (from ___/___/___ to ___/___/___)

PROJECT YEAR 1 2 3 4 Consolidated (please circle)

PERSONNEL:

Name Position Base Salary % Time Total Grant Other Support Support

Fringe Benefits (_____%)

SUBTOTAL $_____

DIRECT COSTS

OFFICE OPERATIONS	$
Supplies	$
Duplicating	$
Telephone and Fax	$
Internet Services	$
Postage and Delivery	$
Equipment Rental	$
Service Agreement(s)	$
Communications/Marketing	$
Software	$
Computer Time	$
Meeting Costs	$
Utilities	$
Travel	$
Insurance	$
Maintenance	$
Leased Space	$
Consultant and Professional Fees	$
Other (specify)	$
SUBTOTAL	$

EQUIPMENT

	$

INDIRECT COSTS

	$
	$

	Committed Funds	Pending Funds
Grants/Contributions/Contracts	$	$
✍ Federal Government	$	$
✍ State Government	$	$
✍ Local Government	$	$
✍ Foundations	$	$
✍ Corporations	$	$
✍ Individual Donors	$	$
✍ Other (specify)	$	$
Income Earned	$	$
✍ Fundraising events	$	$
✍ Capital Campaigns	$	$
✍ Events	$	$
✍ Publications	$	$
✍ Products	$	$
Memberships & Contributions Income	$	$
In-kind Donations & Support (including calculated volunteer time)	$	$
Other (specify)	$	$
Total Revenue	$	$

GRAND TOTAL $_____

Life Cycle of New Grant Application Submitted February 1, 2004

Milestone	Timetable
Application received at Funding Agency	Postmarked 1 February 2004
Receipt sent to applicant	Receipt mailed by agency by 31 March 2004
First Level review by committee	Meeting June 13-14, 2004
Priority Score available	Contact Program Officer by e-mail approximately 7 working days post review.
Summary Statement available	Request Program Officer sends as e-mail attachment in early August 2004 Hardcopy mailed by Agency.
Preliminary Funds Available	As applicable
Second Level review by Board of Regents	Meeting September 10-11, 2004
Funding Agency Staff prepare funding recommendations	End of September—early October 2004
Funding decisions implemented	September-November 2004, depending on availability of funds
Notice of Grant Award mailed by Funding Agency	November—December 2004

GRANT RESOURCES

TEST BEFORE YOU INVEST.

"Test everything. Hold on to the good"
(1 Thessalonians 5:21)

GRANT SEEKERS RESOURCES

Sources of grant monies change frequently depending on the stability of the economy as well as with local, national and global factors. Grant seekers should refer to the following sources of information as a resource tool for future grant funding.

Commerce Business Daily. Superintendent of Documents, U.S. Government Printing Office, Washington, D. C. 20090; (202)512-0000 www.cbd.cos.com

Corporate Giving Watch, Corporate Giving Directory, and Directory of International Corporate Giving in America. Contact: The Taft Group; 1-800-877-TAFT x 1950

Directory of Grant makers Interested in Pre-collegiate Education. Contact: The Council of Foundations, 1828 L Street, N. W., Washington, D. C. 20036; (202) 466-6512. www.cof.org

Federal Register. Superintendent of Documents, U.S. Government Printing Office (see address above).

Foundation Fundamentals: A Guide to Grant seekers by Patricia Reed. Contact: The Foundation Center, 79 Fifth Avenue, Department JC, New York, NY 10003. 1-800-424-9836 www.fdncenter.org

Giving USA and Giving USA Update. Contact: American Association of Fund-Raising Counsel Trust for Philanthropy, 25 West 43rd Street, Suite 1519, New York, NY 10036; (212) 354-5799. *NOTE: Their phone number has changed to (212)-481-6705*

Guide to U. S. Department of Education Programs. Published annually and lists all grant and other programs available from the U. S. Department of Education. Cost: $4.00. Contact: U. S. Government Printing Office (see address above).

National Guide to Funding for Elementary and Secondary Education. Provides profiles of more than 1,400 foundations and corporate direct giving programs that target grades K-12. It includes a comprehensive index and sample grants. Cost: $125. Contact: The Foundation Center, New York, NY; (800)-424-9836.

The Catalog of Federal Domestic Assistance. Complete list of all federal grants allocated by Congress; published annually with occasional up-date supplements. Cost $38. Contact: U. S. Government Printing Office (see address above). www.gsa.gov

The Directory of Computer and Higher Technology Grants. Gives brief entries on 640 organizations for more than 4,000 hardware, software, and high tech-related grants. Cost: $44.50. Contact: Research Grand Guides, Loxahatchee, FL; (561) 795-6129.

The Foundation Directory and National Directory of Corporate Giving. Contact: The Foundation Center, 79 Fifth Avenue, New York, NY 10003; (800) 424-9836. This is one of the most comprehensive sources of information on sources of funds in the U. S. It operates libraries in San Francisco, Cleveland, New York, and Washington, D. C. and maintains collections in 170 libraries across the country. Call the 800 number for the location of collections in your state.

The Local Education Foundation: A New Way to Raise Money for Schools by George Neill. Contact: National Association of Secondary School Principals, 1904 Association Drive, Reston, VA 22091. (703) 860-0200

The Sloane Report. Contact: P. O. Box 561689, Miami, FL, 33256; (305) 251-2199.

The Survey of Corporate Contributions. Contact: The Conference Board, 845 Third Avenue, New York, NY 10022; (212) 759-0900.

Many corporations donate generously to education. The following corporations have in the past, and probably will continue in to future to fund projects, which lead to improved achievement in math, science, and literacy through an educational technology approach. They have also provided hardware, software, other high-tech equipment, and consulting services.

Apple Computer: Provides product donations, some cash grants for innovative uses of computers to grades K-12 in partnership with supermarkets in Apples for the student programs. Contact: Apple Community Affairs Mail Stop 38 J, 20525 Mariani Avenue Cupertino, CA 95014

The Computer Learning Foundation: This non-profit educational foundation promotes effective use of computer technology. It sponsors contests in various subjects using technology to achieve national educational goals or to meet needs of special education students. Contact: The Computer Learning Foundation, P. O. Box 60400 Palo Alto, CA 94036-0400

Hewlett-Packard: Provides funds for projects in K-12, which focus on improving math and science achievement and promoting math and science careers for minorities and women. Contact: Hewlett-Packard Corporate Contributions Program 3000 Hanover Street P. O. Box 10301 Palo Alto, CA 94304

IBM: Provides funding in 12 areas including school system reform, classroom learning, math and science, dropout prevention, school-to-work transition, parent involvement, teacher professional development, literacy, early childhood, drug abuse prevention, economically disadvantaged youth, students with disability and special needs. Contact: IBM Corporate Support Programs Old Orchard Road Armonk, NY 10504

Matsushita Electric Corporation of America: Establishes 5 to 10 year partnerships with school districts and state departments of education to promote systematic school reform, usually through paying consulting fees for educational improvement programs. Contact: Matsushita Electric Corporation of America Corporate Contributions One Panasonic Way 3G 7 Secaucus, NJ 07094

Microsoft Corporation: Provides cash grants, product donations, employee donation matching program, and volunteer outreach to schools, primarily in Washington state. Contact: Microsoft Corporation Attn: Vice-President, Law & Corporate Affairs One Microsoft Way Redmond, WA 98052-6399

NEC: Provides assistance to secondary schools, which emphasize technology education. Contact: NEC Foundation of America Attn: Executive Director 8 Old Sod Farm Road Melville, NY 11747

Toshiba America Information Systems: Provides grants in math and science, product donations, and teacher education in grades 7-12. Contact: President, Toshiba America Foundation 375 Park Avenue New York, NY 10152

Toyota Motor Sales USA, Inc.: Provides funding to math and science programs in K-12; sponsors partnerships between high schools, colleges and universities. Contact: Toyota USA Foundation 19001 South Western Avenue Torrance, CA 90509

Funding is also available for groups interested in designing new American schools and for receiving information related to school reform.

New American Schools Development Corporation (NASDC): This non-profit corporation was designed to "jump-start" the process of developing new American schools. Contact: Toyota USA Foundation or TAPESTRY 1742 Connecticut Avenue N.W. Washington, D.C. 20007

SECTION II

How to get the Grant

CORPORATE LETTER REQUEST

Sample Corporate Letter Request Format

October 2, 2004

INDIVIDUAL'S NAME

Organization's Name
Street Address
City, State, Zip

Dear Mr./Mrs./Ms.:

Open with conciseness and command to capture the Reader's Attention

➢

➢

➢

Introduce Your Organization and How You Can Solve the Problem. Be sure to include program information here along with statistical information. It is essential to include facts, program costs, program goals & objectives, timeframes, etc.

_____

_____

_____

_____

_____

_____

State why your organization is approaching this funding source. Be sure to include the total program budget amount.

_____

_____

_____

_____

_____

_____

Close the Sale (You can either ask for a specific amount or you can leave it open.)

_____

_____

_____

_____

_____

Salutation,

Name of Executive Director
Title

Enclosures

Finishing Touches

Hand write a postscript message here.

Corporate Letter Request Check List

Have you selected the best project for your corporate letter request? ☐ Yes ☐ No

Have you researched a prospective donor list? ☐ Yes ☐ No

Have you contacted the potential funder? ☐ Yes ☐ No

Can you find a challenge or a match? ☐ Yes ☐ No

Are you mailing at the best possible time for optimum response? ☐ Yes ☐ No

Have you created a physical schedule for all phases of production? ☐ Yes ☐ No

Have you budgeted for all expenses? ☐ Yes ☐ No

Have you developed a mailing list? ☐ Yes ☐ No

Have you segmented your list for personalization? ☐ Yes ☐ No

Does the mailing envelope make you want to open it? ☐ Yes ☐ No

Does the mailing envelope meet mailing requirements? (Size, permit#, return address, artwork placement, etc.) ☐ Yes ☐ No

Is it personal at appropriate levels? (Direct imprint vs. label, etc.) ☐ Yes ☐ No

Is the letter eye-catching? ☐ Yes ☐ No

Is the letter interesting to read? ☐ Yes ☐ No

Does the letter demonstrate an emotional appeal? ☐ Yes ☐ No

Does it clearly explain the mission and how the money will be used? ☐ Yes ☐ No

Does it create a sense of urgency and importance? ☐ Yes ☐ No

Does it contain an effective P.S.? ☐ Yes ☐ No

Does it offer payment options (check, credit card, gifts of stock, etc.)? ☐ Yes ☐ No

Does it include matching gift information? ☐ Yes ☐ No

Have you used a courtesy or business reply envelope based? ☐ Yes ☐ No

Are all pieces coordinated? ☐ Yes ☐ No

Does everything physically fit? ☐ Yes ☐ No

Does it really work—have you read it, filled it out, and mailed it back? ☐ Yes ☐ No

Check List Continued…

Has it been proofed by several people before printing? ☐ Yes ☐ No

Is your package environmentally sensitive? ☐ Yes ☐ No

Have you planned received materials for "thank you's"? ☐ Yes ☐ No

Have you communicated to the staff how donors will be tracked? ☐ Yes ☐ No

Have you included project information into your publicity campaign? ☐ Yes ☐ No

Have you strengthened your organization's relationship with members? ☐ Yes ☐ No

Have you delivered on all of your promises? ☐ Yes ☐ No

Have you evaluated the profitability of your program? ☐ Yes ☐ No

FUNDRAISING LETTER

Sample Fund Raising Letter

The following fundraising letter raised over $10,000 in a 3-week period for a battered women's shelter. Although names have been changed to protect the identity of those involved, the letter is real.

Dear Tracy:

The shelter was full, almost to capacity. Children were laughing and playing on the stairs, chase each other and having fun with their new toys. Mothers and a few staff members were sitting in the dining room munching on some scrumptious cookies that someone dropped off. There were cookies, eggnog, and other treats in the refrigerator.

It was Christmas morning.

There was a soft knock at the door. Outside stood a woman and her young daughter who was around 8-years-old. Her face was puffy and her eyes were swollen—from crying or a beating, it was hard to tell. It didn't matter. The mother held a small bundle with one hand and clutched her daughter with the other. The girl's eyes were wide with a strange mixture of curiosity, fear, and relief.

The women in the dining room, warm from sharing a holiday with new friends in a safe place, greeted the woman, got her some food, and wished them both a "Merry Christmas". She thanked them but said she didn't celebrate Christmas. She was Muslim.

Quietly, she mentioned that today was her daughter's birthday. Could they celebrate that?

The women jumped into gear. Holiday paper was taken off a doll that was wrapped with Christmas paper and rewrapped in birthday paper. Someone made a special cake. Everyone sang "Happy Birthday" to the little girl who had run away from her abusive father on her special day.

I tell you that story because I want you to know that every kind of woman, from a wide variety of cultures and backgrounds, comes to us for refuge from violence. And our volunteers and staff do everything in their power to comfort women and children who are forced to leave their homes in fear.

Your generosity makes these rescues possible. Your gift to HPC Shelter will help nearly 400 women and children who will come to us in 2004, looking for a place that is safe from violence, crime, safe from fear, and safe from domestic and child abuse. Thank you.

Sincerely,

Shelter Director

P.S. Share your joy in this holiday season. A $50 gift will give one night's protection for a woman or child who is fleeing for their lives from a dangerous place. Your generous gift will help women and children build new lives in peace while gaining a sense of dignity, increasing their self-esteem, and feeling secure.

COMMON GRANT APPLICATION

DONORS FORUM OF WISCONSIN

COMMON APPLICATION FORM

Revised as of March 2004

The Common Application Form is to be used for all types of proposals: special projects, capital and general operating support. Please note that there are some differences in the information required, depending upon the type of request.

A list of the funders who have agreed to accept this form is attached. Please keep in mind that **every funder has different guidelines, priorities, application procedures and timelines** (i.e., some of the funders may also require letters of intent prior to submission of full proposals; others may fund only in certain fields; some funders may require more than one copy.)

Information about individual grant programs is available from each funder, the **Donors Forum of Wisconsin** (414/270-1978 fax: 414/270-1979) and at the **Marquette University Funding Information Center**. Marquette University Memorial Library: (phone 414/288-1515) or web site at http://www.marquette.edu/library/fic. Additional copies of the Common Application may be requested from the Donors Forum of Wisconsin and Marquette's Funding Information Center.

GENERAL INSTRUCTIONS

- Type and single-space all proposals. (minimum 10 point)

- Provide all of the information in the order listed.

- All questions relative to the request must be completed fully.

- Submit only one copy with numbered pages; do not bind or staple.

- Do not include materials other than those specifically requested at this time.

- Do not send videotapes.

Submit the following attachments with the completed proposal:

1. Complete list of the organization's officers and directors

2. The organization's actual income and expense statement for the **past** fiscal year, identifying the organization's principal sources of support

3. The organization's projected income and expense budget for the **current** fiscal year, identifying the projected revenue sources

4. The organization's most recent audited financial statement including notes and IRS Form 990

5. Copies of the IRS federal tax exemption determination letters

For specific questions on the Common Grant Application and a schedule for Grant seeker Workshops please call the Donors Forum of Wisconsin at (414) 270-1978.

Grant makers that Accept the

Common Application Form

March 2004

The following funders have agreed to accept the Common Application Form. Other funders, not listed, may also accept the Common Application Form. **Before sending an application to any funder, be sure to check for their specific requirements**. For a complete list of Wisconsin Foundations please refer to FOUNDATIONS IN WISCONSIN: A DIRECTORY—Funding Information Center, Marquette University—Memorial Library (414) 228-1515.

- Aid Association for Lutherans
- Ameritech
- Ashley Foundation
- Elizabeth A. Brinn Foundation
- The Brico Fund
- City of Milwaukee
- Emory T. Clark Family Charitable Foundation
- Patrick & Anna M. Cudahy Fund
- Derse Family Foundation
- Elizabeth Elser Doolittle Charitable Trusts
- Barbara Meyer Elsner Foundation
- Bucyrus-Erie Foundation
- Ralph Evinrude Foundation
- Fleck Foundation
- Foundation of Faith (required for grant requests over $10,000)
- Fortis Insurance Foundation

- Gardner Foundation
- Harley-Davidson Foundation
- Charles E. & Dorothy W. Inbusch Foundation
- J. T. Jacobus Family Foundation
- R. G. Jacobus Family Foundation
- Kohler Foundation
- Faye McBeath Foundation
- Milwaukee Foundation
- Northwestern Mutual Life Foundation
- Jane B. Pettit Foundation
- St. Anthony's Foundation
- Siebert Lutheran Foundation
- Stackner Family Foundation
- United Performing Arts Fund
- United Way of Greater Milwaukee
- Wisconsin Energy Corp. Foundation
- Ziemann Foundation

COMMON APPLICATION FORM

Provide the following grant information in this order. For your convenience, you may choose either to copy and fill out this cover summary, create your own using the headings listed below or download the form from the Funding Information Center, Marquette University's web site: ttp://www.marquette.edu/library/fic

Funder applying to: _____

Date Submitted: _____

Total Proposed Project/Program Budget: _____

Amount Requested: _____

Program Name: _____

Duration of Project/Program: from: _____ to: _____

When are funds needed? _____

Nature of Request: _____ capital _____ project _____ operating _____ program _____ endowment _____ other

---

Organization Information:

Name and address:

Phone number: _____ TTY: _____ FAX number: _____

Email: _____ FEI #: _____ Date of Incorporation: _____

Chief Staff Officer/Title: _____ Phone number: _____

Contact Person/Title: _____ Phone number: _____

Board Chairperson/Title: _____

Dates of organization's fiscal year: ____

Organization's total operating budget for past year _____ and current year _____

Has the governing board approved a policy, which states that the organization does not discriminate as to age, race, religion, sex or national origin?

yes___ no___ When? _____

Does the organization have federal tax-exempt status? _____ yes _____ no

If no, please explain

Has the organization's chief executive officer authorized this request?

_____ yes _____ no

An officer of the organization's governing body must sign this application:

The undersigned, an authorized officer of the organization, does hereby certify that the information set forth in this grant application is true and correct, that the Federal tax exemption determination letter attached hereto has not been revoked and the present operation of the organization and its current sources of support are not inconsistent with the organization's continuing tax exempt classification as set forth in such determination letter.

_____

Signature   **Date**

_____

Print Name/Title   **Date**

Enclose all required support materials with the application (see page 1 General Instructions).

NARRATIVE

Please provide the following information in the order presented below. Note sections that are not required for general operating support. Refer to the glossary of terms as needed when preparing the narrative.

(No more than five pages; ten point minimum; one inch borders; include applicant's name on the top of each page)

Project/Program Abstract (not required for general operating requests)

Describe in three to five sentences the proposed program, how it relates to the organization's mission, capacity to carry out the program and who will benefit from the program.

Organization Information

Provide a brief summary of the organization:

- mission, goals, programs, and major accomplishments, success stories and qualifications;
- show evidence of client & community support
- description of the population served, including total number, geographic, demographic,
- and socio/economic characteristics
- total number of paid staff and volunteers (differentiate between board members, program and office volunteers)

Project/Program Description (not required for general operating requests)

- Explain the significance/scope of the program and why your organization is qualified to carry it out.
- Describe the expected outcomes and the indicators of those outcomes.
- Describe the evaluation process and how the results will be used.
- Document the size and characteristics of the population to be served.
- Outline the strategy/methodology and timeline to be used in the development and implementation of the program.
- What linkages/collaborations will be used?

- How do you plan to involve the population you intend to serve in the design?

- How does this program enhance the existing services in the community?

Funding Considerations

Describe plans for obtaining other funding needed to carry out the project/program or organizational goals, including amounts requested of other funders. If the project/program is expected to continue beyond the grant period, describe plans for ensuring continued funding after the grant period. List the top five funders of this project (if applying for a program grant) or organization (if applying for general operating support) in the previous fiscal year, the current year, and those pending for the next fiscal year.

Common Application

> **Send a capital budget if you are requesting capital support.**

PROJECT/PROGRAM BUDGET

ORGANIZATION NAME: _____

PROJECT/PROGRAM REVENUE

	Total Revenue	Committed	Pending
1. United Way Allocation	$	$	$
2. Other Federated Campaign Allocations	$	$	$
3. Contracts (list specific sources on following page)	$	$	$
4. Grants (list sources on following page: Foundations, Corporations & Government)	$	$	$
5. In-Kind Support (list specific sources on following page)	$	$	$

6. Client and
    Program Service
    Fees and Other $ _____ $ _____ $ _____
    Earned Revenue

7. Contributions
    (Gifts from $ _____ $ _____ $ _____
    Individuals)

8. Other Revenue
    (list specific
    sources on
    following page $ _____ $ _____ $ _____
    including any
    endowment
    income)

TOTAL $ _____ $ _____ $ _____
PROJECT/PROGRAM
REVENUE

PROGRAM/PROJECT EXPENSES

1. Salaries (provide detail by position on a
    separate page, <u>except for United Way
    applications)</u> $ _____

2. Benefits/Taxes $ _____

3. Professional Fees (itemize on following
    page) $ _____

4. Supplies, Printing, Duplicating $ _____

5. Travel $ _____

6. Telephone $ _____

7. Occupancy $ _____

8. Payments to Affiliates $ _____

9. Program/Project specific major property
    & equipment Acquisition $ _____

10. In kind Expenses $ _____

11. Other Expenses (itemize on following
    page) $ _____

TOTAL PROJECT/PROGRAM EXPENSES $ _____

(Please note: revenue and expenses should add up to total project revenue and expenses.)

PROJECT/PROGRAM REVENUE SUPPLEMENT

(Please indicate revenue sources as committed or pending)

Use additional sheet if necessary

Contracts (list)	Total Revenue	Committed	Pending
_____	_____	_____	_____
_____	_____	_____	_____
_____	_____	_____	_____
_____	_____	_____	_____

Grants (list)	Total Revenue	Committed	Pending
_____	_____	_____	_____
_____	_____	_____	_____
_____	_____	_____	_____
_____	_____	_____	_____

In-Kind Support (list)	Total Revenue	Committed	Pending
_____	_____	_____	_____
_____	_____	_____	_____
_____	_____	_____	_____
_____	_____	_____	_____

Other (list)	Total Revenue	Committed	Pending
_____	_____	_____	_____
_____	_____	_____	_____
_____	_____	_____	_____
_____	_____	_____	_____

PROJECT/PROGRAM EXPENSES SUPPLEMENT

Use additional sheet if necessary

Salaries (Detail by position)

_____

_____

_____

_____

Other Expenses (list)

_____

_____

_____

_____

Professional Fees (list)

_____

_____

_____

_____

_____

In-kind Expenses (list)

_____

_____

_____

_____

_____

NATIONAL NETWORK OF GRANT MAKERS

COMMON GRANT APPLICATION

NNG

NATIONAL NETWORK OF GRANTMAKERS

Common Grant Application

Dear Nonprofit Colleague:

To save you time and effort in the grant application process, the National Network of Grant makers (NNG) has developed this common application form. NNG is an organization of grant makers committed to social justice and philanthropic reform. The common application format is one way of moving toward our mission.

Strategies for Successful Grant Seeking:

- a copy of its annual report and/or guidelines.

- Familiarize yourself with the funder's application process, including timetable and preferred method of initial contact. It is important to note that some funders accept proposals only after an initial phone call, query letter or pre-application form and in general, it is never a good idea to send out mass mailing of proposals.

- Include a brief cover letter that outlines the link between your proposal and the funder's interests. One paragraph of the cover letter should provide a brief summary of your project.

- Follow the attached format and any specific instructions from the funder.

- Remember that NNG members are interested in addressing the root causes of social problems and address this in your narrative.

Because this is a broad attempt to meet the general requirements of a number of grant makers, certain funders might request additional information.

The National Network of Grant makers is an organization of individuals involved in funding social and economic justice. The Network values individuals, projects and organizations working for systemic change in the U.S. and abroad, in order to create an equitable distribution of wealth and power and mutual respect for all peoples. NNG works primarily within organized philanthropy to increase financial and other resources to groups committed to social and economic justice. NNG has three strategic directions: Embarking on a campaign to galvanize existing and new philanthropic resources for social and economic justice work; Providing a network to offer mutual support for progressive grant makers, share information across grant making sectors and promote the exchange of information and strategies among social change funders and community activists; Working to reshape philanthropic policies and procedures among our own members, as well as the larger field of philanthropy, to promote diversity and open, democratic processes in order to increase the amount of funding and other resources for progressive social change.

For more information contact:
NNG, 1717 Kettner Boulevard, # 110, San Diego,CA 92101
Tel (619) 231-1348 Fax (619) 231-1349 E-mail:nng@nng.org
Web site:www.nng.org

This Common Grant Application is a project of the National Network of Grantmakers. The form consists of five pages: a cover letter, Participating Funders List, Cover Sheet & Narrative Instructions and Budget page. If any pages are missing, please request them from your source for this form.

Participating Funders List

Information about individual foundation funding interests is available from each funder. The NNG *Grantmakers Directory* is a good starting place for this type of information. It can be obtained from NNG. Please call for the current price. In addition, many local libraries carry a collection of funding resources provided by the Foundation Center. To identify a participating library near you, please call the Foundation Center at (800) 424-9836 or access their web site at http://www.fdncenter.org.

Foundations accepting the NNG Common Grant Application:*

A Territory Resource
Abelard Foundation-East
Abelard Foundation-West
Acorn Foundation
Jennifer Altman Foundation
Amazon Foundation
Angelica Foundation
Susan A. & Donald P. Babson Charitable Foundation
Beldon Fund
Ben & Jerry's Foundation
Boehm Foundation
Boston Globe Foundation
Bridge Builders Foundation
C.S. Fund
CarEth Foundation
Changemakers
Chicago Resource Center
Chinook Fund
Discount Foundation
Episcopal City Mission
FACT Services Company, Inc. for the French American Charitable Trust
Foundation for Mid South
Fund for Nonviolence
Fund for Southern Communities
Fund of the Four Directions
Funding Exchange
Wallace Alexander Gerbode Foundation
Gill Foundation
Greensboro Justice Fund
HKH Foundation
Jadetree Two Foundation

Larson Legacy
Liberty Hill Foundation
Marianist Sharing Fund
McKay Foundation
Bert & Mary Meyer Foundation
Charles Stewart Mott Foundation
Stewart R.Mott Charitable Trust
Stewart R.Mott's Building Organized Community Program
A.J.Muste Memorial Institute
Needmor Fund
Nokomis Foundation
Jessie Smith Noyes Foundation
Ottinger Foundation
Peace Development Fund
Prospect Hill Foundation
Public Welfare Foundation
Rockefeller Family Fund
San Diego Foundation for Change
Sapelo Foundation
Seva Foundation
Seventh Generation Fund
Shefa Fund
Ralph L. Smith Foundation
Solidago Foundation
Southern Partners Fund
Stern Family Fund
Sun Hill Foundation
Tides Foundation
Unitarian Universalist Funding Program
Unitarian Universalist Veatch Program at Shelter Rock
Rose & Sherle Wagner Foundation
Women's Peacepower Foundation

*It is best to contact funders before submitting your application.

Common Grant Application Formats Available

The NNG Common Grant Application is also available in Braille, on diskette and at the Foundation Center and Hands Net sites on the web. Please contact the NNG office for more information.

La versión en español está disponible de parte de la Red Nacional de Donantes/Fundaciones (NNG). No todas las fundaciones aceptan esta versión. Vea pagina

The Spanish language version is available from the National Network of Grantmakers (NNG). Not all foundations accept this version. See page four.

This Common Grant Application is a project of the National Network of Grantmakers. The form consists of five pages: a cover letter, Participating Funders List, Cover Sheet & Narrative Instructions and Budget page. If any pages are missing, please request them from your source for this form.

I. COVER SHEET (PLEASE USE THIS FORMAT TO CREATE A ONE-PAGE COVER SHEET.)

Organization Name: _____

Tax exempt status: _____Year organization was founded: _____

Date of application: _____

Address: _____

Telephone number: _____Fax number: _____

Director: _____

Contact person and title (if not director): _____

Grant request: _____Period grant will cover: _____

Type of request (general support, start-up, technical assistance, etc.): _____

Project title (if project funding is requested): _____

Total project budget (if request is for other than general support): _____

Total organizational budget (current year): _____

Starting date of fiscal year: _____

Summarize the organization's mission (two to three sentences): _____

_____

_____

Summary of project or grant request (two to three sentences): _____

_____

_____

II.   NARRATIVE (MAXIMUM OF FIVE PAGES.)

A.   Introduction and Background of Organization (Incorporating the following points:)

1.   Briefly describe your organization's history and major accomplishments.

2.   Describe your current programs and activities.

3.   Who is your constituency (be specific about demographics such as race, class, gender, ethnicity, age, sexual orientation and people with disabilities)? How are they actively involved in your work and how do they benefit from this program and/or your organization?

4.   If you are a grassroots group, describe your community. If you are a state, regional or national organization, describe your work with local groups, if applicable and how other regional and/or national organizations are involved.

B.   Describe Your Request (Incorporating the following points:)

1.   Problem statement: what problems, needs or issues does it address?

2.   If other than general operating support, describe the program for which you seek funding, why you decided to pursue this project and whether it is a new or ongoing part of your organization.

3.   What are the goals, objectives and activities/strategies involved in this request? Describe your specific activities/strategies using a timeline over the course of this request.

4.   How does your work promote diversity and address inequality, oppression and discrimination within your organization as well as the larger society?

5. Describe systemic or social change you are trying to achieve: How does your work address and change the underlying or root causes of the problem?

III. ATTACHMENTS/REQUIREMENTS (SUPPLY EVERYTHING CHECKED BELOW BY FUNDER WHO PREPARED THIS COPY.)

A. Evaluation

☐ 1. Briefly describe your plan for evaluating the success of the project or for your organization's work. What questions will be addressed? Who will be involved in evaluating this work—staff, board, constituents, community, consultants? How will the evaluation results be used?

B. Organizational Structure/Administration

☐ 1. Briefly describe how your organization works: What are the responsibilities of board, staff and volunteers? And if membership organization, define criteria for membership. Are there dues?

☐ 2. Who will be involved in carrying out the plans outlined in this request? Include a brief paragraph summarizing the qualifications of key individuals involved.

☐ 3. Provide a list of your board of directors with related demographic information.

☐ 4. How is the board selected, who selects them and how often?

☐ 5. Include an organizational chart showing decision-making structure.

C. Finances

☐ 1. Most recent, completed full year organizational financial statement (expenses, revenue and balance sheet), audited, if available.

☐ 2. Organization's current annual operating budget (See attached budget format).

☐ 3. Current project budget, other than general support (See attached format).

☐ 4. Projected operating budget for upcoming year (See attached format).

☐ 5. List individually other funding sources for this request. Include amounts and whether received, committed or projected/pending.

☐ 6.   Describe your plans for future fund raising.

☐ 7.   A copy of your IRS 501(c)(3) letter. If you do not have 510(c)(3) status, check with the funder to see if they are willing to fund through your fiscal sponsor or are willing to exercise expenditure responsibility. Additional information may be required to do so.

☐ 8.   Other

D. Other Supporting Material

☐ 1.   Letters of support/commitment (up to three).

☐ 2.   Recent newsletter articles, newspaper clippings, evaluations or reviews (up to three).

☐ 3.   Recent annual report.

☐ 4.   Videos/cassettes are accepted ONLY if this box is checked.

☐ 5.   Other

Guidelines for applicants (completed by funder)

Send __ number of complete copies: cover sheet, five page proposal and attachments that are checked off.

Use a standard typeface no smaller than 10 points and no less than .25 in margins.

Proposals by fax are ☐are not ☐ accepted.

Binders or folders are ☐ are not ☐ accepted.

Your proposal must be ☐ double sided ☐ single sided ☐ no preference.

Please use the following paper: ☐ white/very light colored   ☐ recycled

☐ 8½ x11 inches only   ☐ no preference

Sí, aceptamos las solicitudes de fondos en español.   ☐Yes, we accept funding proposals in Spanish.

No aceptamos las solicitudes en español.   ☐ No, we do not accept funding proposals in Spanish.

Funder who prepared this copy of the Common Grant Application: _____

IV. BUDGET

If you already prepare organizational and project budgets that approximate this format, please feel free to submit them in their original forms. You may reproduce this form on your computer and/or submit separate pages for income and expenses.

Budget for the period: _____ to_____

	EXPENSES			INCOME	
Item	Amount	FT/PT		Source	Amount

Salaries & wages

Government grants & (breakdown by contracts (specify) individual position and indicate $Foundations (specify) full or part-time)

Corporations

Religious Institutions

United Way, Combined

Fringe benefits & payroll Taxes

Federal Campaign & other federated campaigns

Consultants & professional fees

Travel

Individual contributions

Equipment

Fundraising events

Supplies & products

Training

Membership income

Printing & copying

In-kind support

Telephone & fax

Other (earned income, consulting fees, etc. Please specify.)

Postage & delivery

Rent & utilities

In-kind expense

Other (specify)

TOTAL EXPENSE $_____   TOTAL INCOME $_____

                                        BALANCE $_____

This Common Grant Application is a project of the National Network of Grantmakers. The form consists of five pages: a cover letter, Participating Funders List, Cover Sheet & Narrative Instructions and Budget page. If any pages are missing, please request them from your source for this form.

STRATEGIC PLANNING & ORGANIZA-
TIONAL ASSESSMENT WORKSHEETS

Strategic Planning Regarding the Total Organization

Rating *	Indicator	Met	Needs Work	N/A
E	1. The organization's purpose and activities meet community needs.			
R	2. The organization frequently evaluates, by soliciting community input, whether its mission and activities provide benefit to the community.			
R	3. The organization has a value statement that is reflected in the agency's activities and is communicated by its constituents.			
A	4. The value statement includes standards of ethical behavior and respect for other's interests.			
E	5. The organization has a clear, meaningful written mission statement, which reflects its purpose, values and people served.			
R	6. The board and staff periodically review the mission statement and modify it to reflect changes in the environment.			
E	7. The board and staff developed and adopted a written strategic plan to achieve its mission.			
A	8. Board, staff, service recipients, volunteers, key constituents and general members of the community participate in the planning process.			
E	9. The plan was developed by researching the internal and external environment.			
R	10. The plan identifies the changing community needs including the agency's strengths, weaknesses, opportunities and threats.			
R	11. The planning process identifies the critical issues facing the organization.			
R	12. The plan sets goals and measurable objectives that address these critical issues.			
E	13. The plan integrates all the organization's activities around a focused mission.			
R	14. The plan prioritizes the agency goals and develops timelines for their accomplishments.			
A	15. The plan establishes an evaluation process and performance indicators to measure the progress toward the achievement of goals and objectives.			
R	16. Through work plans, human and financial resources are allocated to insure the accomplishment of the goals in a timely fashion.			
A	17. The plan is communicated to all stakeholders of the agency—service recipients, board, staff, volunteers and the general community.			
Indicators ratings: E=essential; R=recommended; A=additional to strengthen organizational activities				

Strategic **Planning** Regarding the Organization's Programs

Rating *	Indicator	Met	Needs Work	N/A
E	1. Programs are congruent with the agency's mission and strategic plan.			
A	2. The organization actively informs the public about its programs and services.			
A	3. Clients and potential clients have the opportunity to participate in program development.			
R	4. Sufficient resources are allocated to ensure each program can achieve the established goals and objectives.			
R	5. Staff has sufficient training and skill level to produce the program.			
A	6. Programs within the organization are integrated to provide more complete services to clients.			
R	7. Each program has performance indicators to insure that the program meets its goals and objectives.			
R	8. Performance indicators are reviewed annually.			
A	9. The agency networks and/or collaborates with other organizations to produce the most comprehensive and effective services to clients.			

Indicators ratings: E=essential; R=recommended; A=additional to strengthen organizational activities

Planning Regarding the Organization's Evaluations

Rating *	Indicator	Met	Needs Work	N/A
R	1. Every year, the organization evaluates its activities to determine progress toward goal accomplishment.			
A	2. Stakeholders are involved in the evaluation process.			
R	3. The evaluation includes a review of organizational programs and systems to insure that they comply with the organization's mission, values and goals.			
R	4. The results of the evaluation are reflected in the revised plan.			
A	5. Periodically, the organization conducts a comprehensive evaluation of its programs. This evaluation measures program outcomes.			
Indicators ratings: E=essential; R=recommended; A=additional to strengthen organizational activities				

GRANTS MANAGEMENT SYSTEM

PROSPECT WORKSHEET

Date:		
Basic Information		
Name		
Address		
Contact Person		
Financial Data		
Total Assets		
Total Grants Paid		
Grant Ranges/Amount Needed		
Period of Funding/Project		
Is Funder a Good Match?	**Funder**	**Your Organization**
Subject Focus (list in order of importance)	1.	1.
	2.	2.
	3.	3.
Geographic Limits		
Type(s) of Support		
Population(s) Served		
Type(s) of Recipients		
People (Officers, Donors, Trustees, Staff)		
Application Information		
Does the funder have printed guidelines/application forms?		
Initial Approach (letter of inquiry, formal proposal)		
Deadline(s)		
Board Meeting Date(s)		
Sources of Above Information		
☐ 990-PF—Year:	☐ Requested ☐ Received	
☐ Annual Report—Year:	☐ Requested ☐ Received	
☐ Directories/grant indexes		
☐ Grantmaker Web site		
Notes:		
Follow up:		

Prospect Worksheet-Individual Donors

Basic Information
Name (first, middle, last):
Title (Mr., Ms., Mrs., Dr.):
Former or maiden name or nickname:
Address:
Phone number(s):
Alternate address:

Employment Information
Place of Employment:
Web site (if any): http://
Address:
Work phone number:
Work e-mail:
Position (title):
Since (date):
Salary and other benefits (estimated):
Other relevant employment-related data (former employment):

Personal Information
School(s) attended:
Board affiliation(s):
Foundation affiliation(s) (if any):
Civic/volunteer interests:
Social (include club memberships):
Hobbies:
Giving history (include large gifts, dates, etc.):
Assets (real estate, stock, etc.):
Other wealth indicators:

Family Information (if applicable)
Spouse's name:
Spouse's occupation:
Spouse's affiliation(s):
Spouse's philanthropy:
Children's school(s):

Connection to your organization
Board member (dates):
Volunteer (current?):
Current or past donor (amount and other details):
Friend of board member or staff (provide contact name):
Other (shared interests, etc.):

Area(s) of commonality with the prospect
Prior giving history:
Geography:
Subject field:
People:
Other:

Sources consulted (provide URLs, dates, and other details)
Search engines (terms used):
Web sites:
Databases:
Contribution lists:
Directories:
Newspapers:
Other:

History of past cultivation (if any)
Type (letter, call, invitation, meeting, etc., and dates):

Recommended next step(s)
(Indicate deadlines):

SECTION III

Where to get the Grant

GRANT SEEKERS RESOURCES II

Sources of grant monies change frequently depending on the stability of the economy as well as with local, national and global factors. Grant seekers should refer to the following sources of information as a resource tool for future grant funding.

GRANTS FOR NONPROFITS

COMPUTER TECHNOLOGY

AT&T Foundation
http://www.att.com/foundation/
The AT&T Foundation invests globally in projects that are at the intersection of community needs and AT&T's business interests. In general, AT&T Foundation grants support (1) education, (2)arts and culture, (3) civic and community service, and (4) local initiatives.
Also listed under Education.

Beaumont Foundation of America
http://www.bmtfoundation.com/bfa/us/public/en/grants/
Provides state-of-the-art, wireless laptop computers and technology equipment to schools and community groups serving low-income populations and individuals.

Best Buy Children's Foundation
Te@ch Program Grants
http://communications.bestbuy.com/communityrelations/teach.asp?kiosk=
Provides grants in support of school programs or projects that creatively integrate interactive technology into the curriculum.

Best Buy Te@ch Grants
http://www.bestbuy.com/
The Best Buy's Children's Foundation is committed to supporting programs that connect kids, technology and education. Best Buy's te@ch™ program was created to recognize and reward schools that are integrating interactive technology into the curriculum.

Cisco Systems Inc. Philanthropy and Community Giving
http://www.cisco.com/en/US/about/ac48/
about_cisco_community_and_philanthropy_home.html
Cisco Systems pursues its philanthropic goals through three initiatives: workforce development, with a focus on investments in technology and training that help people develop skills to enter or re-enter today's workforce; partnerships with nonprofits that give them access to technology solutions; and helping employees to become successful volunteers and informed philanthropists.

Community Technology Center's Network
http://www.ctcnet.org/
"We are a national, non-profit membership organization of more than one thousand independent community technology centers where people get free or low-cost access to computers and computer-related technology, such as the Internet, together with learning opportunities that encourage exploration and discovery".

Compumentor's TechSoup
http://www.techsoup.org/
A one-stop resource for anything and everything having to do with technology created expressly for nonprofits. TechSoup, a new service from CompuMentor, promises to offer nonprofits clear, non-commercial recommendations for the best places to acquire donated or discounted software; equipment; advice on technology funding; technology planning; computer training; and listings of volunteers and consultants available to assist them.

Computers for Kids
http://www.c4k.org/
Individuals and organizations donate computers that can be used by schools.

Computers for Learning (GSA)
http://www.computers.fed.gov/School/user.asp
The CFL program places computers in our classrooms and prepares our children to contribute and compete in the 21st century. The program transfers excess Federal computer equipment to schools and educational nonprofit organizations, giving special consideration to those with the greatest need.

Donating Used Computers
http://web.archive.org/web/20011004152523/
http://www.cof.org/foundationnews/1100/computers.htm

In addition to exploring the pros and cons of donating computers, provides a list of organizations that accept computers for refurbishing for nonprofits.

Electronic Data Systems Technology Grants
http://www.eds.com/community_affairs/com_tech_grants.shtml
http://www.eds.com/community_affairs/com_overview.shtml
The EDS Technology Grant program helps schoolteachers of children ages 6 through 18 purchase information technology products and services that will improve their pupils' ability to learn. Each year, EDS accounts worldwide sponsor and award $1,500 (U.S. dollars) grants to teachers through a competitive application process.

Foundation for Rural Education and Development (FRED)
http://www.fred.org/
The mission of the Foundation for Rural Education and Development (FRED), a charitable foundation affiliated with the Organization for the Promotion and Advancement of Small Telecommunications Companies (OPASTCO), is to promote activities that improve rural educational, social, and economic conditions.

Gates Foundation (Bill and Melinda)
http://www.gatesfoundation.org/
Bill and Melinda Gates hope to make an enduring contribution toward increasing access to innovations in education, technology, and global health. More than seventeen billion dollars in endowments have been set aside for these causes.

Hardware Donation Programs
http://www.techsoup.org/articlepage.cfm?ArticleId=212&topicid=1
Who to hit up for donated equipment. Advice from TechSoup.

Help Us Help Foundation
http://www.helpushelp.org
With financial support provided by database software giant Oracle Corporation, the nonprofit Help Us Help Foundation assists K-12 public schools and youth organizations in economically challenged communities to obtain information technology tools. Grants of computer equipment and software are available to schools and youth organizations in the U.S. that provide educational programs in low-income communities.

Hewlett-Packard Philanthropy
http://h21030.www2.hp.com/

HP is recognized as a philanthropic leader among global corporations. In 2003, HP contributed more than $62 million in resources worldwide to advance the ability of students, teachers, community residents and nonprofits to solve some of their most fundamental challenges.

Hewlett-Packard Technology for Teaching Grant Initiative
http://grants.hp.com/us/programs/tech_teaching/index.html
HP recently announced a $10 million Technology for Teaching Grant initiative targeting schools in the United States from kindergarten through university level. The initiative is designed to support innovative and effective uses of technology in classrooms so that students may reach their full potential, particularly in math, science and engineering…

Intel Corporate Contributions Program
http://www.intel.com/community/
Intel, the world's largest chip maker, makes direct charitable contributions to nonprofit organizations in the form of donated equipment and products, fellowships and scholarship funds, general/operating support, program development, research, and technical assistance.

Kresge Foundation Challenge Grants
http://www.kresge.org/programs/
A challenge grant program to upgrade and endow scientific instrumentation and laboratories in colleges and universities, teaching hospitals, medical schools, and research institutions. Scientific equipment and attendant renovation of space necessary to accommodate such equipment are eligible projects. Items may include new, replacement, or upgraded equipment and may range from basic science instrumentation for classroom laboratories to a single piece of equipment for student/faculty research. Provides one-fourth of the total project costs. The minimum Kresge grant is $100,000 and the maximum is $500,000.

Magic Johnson Foundation Technology Initiative
http://magicjohnson.org/Tech_about.htm
The Magic Johnson Foundation Technology Initiative is a program that has been created provide technology access and education to inner-city communities. It is our intent to work in conjunction with program partners and sponsors to provide not only access, but also education regarding Information Technology to the underserved urban population.

Microsoft Corporation Community Affairs

http://www.microsoft.com/giving/

Redmond, Washington-based Microsoft makes grants of cash, software, and technical support to nonprofit organizations worldwide in order to help bring the benefits of information technology to people and communities, provide support to organizations in communities in which its employees live and work, and support its employees taking an active role in their community through volunteer and matching-gift programs.

The Mid-Continent Research for Education and Learning (McREL)
Funding for Technology in Education

http://www.mcrel.org/lesson%2Dplans/techined.asp

One of the most difficult aspects of implementing technology in schools is finding and getting the funds for new technologies and associated ongoing expenses. This page brings together reports; funding strategies used by states, districts, and schools; grant writing tools; and funding sources.

NEC Foundation of America

http://www.necfoundation.org/

Makes cash grants to nonprofit organizations and programs with national reach and impact in one or both of the following arenas: science and technology education, principally at the secondary level, and/or the application of technology to assist people with disabilities.

Oracle Help Us Help Foundation

http://www.helpushelp.org/

This nonprofit organization provides assistance to K-12 public schools and youth organizations in economically challenged communities through grants of computer equipment and software. The goal of the program is to ensure that all children have access to Internet technology, and to the learning opportunities that will enable them to succeed in the information age. For more information contact: Ms. Emmanuelle Pancaldi, 650-607-0301, email: HelpUsHelp_us@oracle.com.

PEP National Directory of Computer Recycling Programs

http://web.archive.org/web/20030713042128/

http://microweb.com/pepsite/Recycle/recycle_index.html

A state, national and international directory of agencies that facilitate donations of used computer hardware for schools and community groups sponsored by Resources for Parents, Educators, and Publishers (PEP).

SBC Foundation
http://www.sbc.com/gen/corporate-citizenship?pid=2560
The SBC Foundation, the charitable giving arm of telecommunications giant SBC Communications, places primary emphasis on supporting education programs and initiatives that help increase access to information technologies; broaden technology training and skills development; and effectively integrate new technologies to enhance education and economic development—especially for underserved populations.

SBC Foundation Excelerator Project
http://www.sbc.com/gen/press-room?pid=5097&cdvn=news&newsarticleid=21039
The SBC Foundation—the philanthropic arm of SBC Communications Inc.—has increased its SBC Excelerator technology grant program to a total of $28 million. In 2004, $9 million is available to national and local nonprofit organizations for projects that use technology to build stronger communities.

Schools Online
http://www.schoolsonline.org/
Schools Online will use a $3 million challenge grant to match cash and stock contributions as part of its "Hello 2000" campaign, to expand the group's Internet equipment-donation program to schools around the world...

Second Byte Foundation
http://www.2ndbyte.org/
The Second Byte Foundation exists to identify at-risk children who will benefit from a donated computer system in their homes.

Share the Technology
http://sharetechnology.org/
A non-profit organization in New Jersey dedicated to helping schools obtain used computer equipment.

Teacher Laptop Foundation
http://www.teacherlaptop.org/
A national 501(c)(3) nonprofit charitable organization collecting donations to provide laptops to teachers.

Techlearning.com Grants and Contests
http://www.techlearning.com/grants.html

Provides a directory of awards, grants, and funding opportunities available for schools and teachers.

Technology Grants for Grassroots Organizations
http://www.progressivetech.org
The Organizing Technology Grants Program is designed to help community organizing groups support and develop strategic uses of technology that strengthen their ability to affect change in their communities and beyond.

Technology Opportunities Program (TOP)
http://www.ntia.doc.gov/top
The TOP program funded by the Department of Commerce offers matching grants to state, local, and tribal governments and nonprofit entities that demonstrate innovative uses of digital network technologies. For more information contact: Stephen J. Downs, 202-482-2048, fax 202-501-5136, email: sdowns@ntia.doc.gov.

TechSoup Discount Software for Nonprofits
http://www.techsoup.org/DiscounTech/faq.asp#general
Offesr very inexpensive pricing on software from Microsoft, Symantec, Lotus, WebGecko, B2P, Intuit, and others.

Time Warner Foundation
http://www.aoltimewarnerfoundation.org/
The AOL Time Warner Foundation is dedicated to using the power of media, communications, and information technology to serve the public interest and strengthen society.

Verizon Foundation
http://foundation.verizon.com/
The Verizon Foundation is committed to supporting programs and projects that create innovative e-solutions, help bridge the digital divide, foster basic and computer literacy and help enrich our communities, educate our citizens and create a skilled workforce. The Verizon Foundation looks to forge and maintain partnerships around technology initiatives with local, regional, national and international organizations serving the needs of racial and ethnic communities, people with disabilities, and the economically and socially disadvantaged.

GRANTS FOR NONPROFITS

CHILDREN AND YOUTH

7-Eleven Community Outreach Programs
http://www.7-eleven.com/about/outreachprograms.asp
7-Eleven supports non-profits, libraries, and schools particularly in the following areas: (1) Education is our signature cause, specifically programs that assist adolescents and adults (ages 14 and above) with: Workforce Development and Language Education. 7-Eleven is especially interested in programs that assist at-risk and economically disadvantaged individuals. (2) The company also supports educational programs that recognize the rich cultural diversity in our communities and promote better understanding and tolerance among cultures throughout America. 7-Eleven has a specific interest in programs that serve ethnic and inner-city constituents. (3) 7-Eleven supports programs designed to prevent crime and build stronger, safer and more caring communities, with a special interest in youth-related programs. (4) 7-Eleven also supports the fight against hunger, providing by in-kind contributions of fresh foods to pre-selected food banks in markets where 7-Eleven operates.
Normal grants fall in the $1000-$2500 range and are not renewable.

Administration for Children and Families
http://www.acf.dhhs.gov/
The Administration for Children and Families (ACF) is a federal agency funding state, local, and tribal organizations to provide family assistance (welfare), child support, child care, Head Start, child welfare, and other programs relating to children and families.

Administration for Children and Families
National Child Welfare Resource Center Funding
http://a257.g.akamaitech.net/7/257/2422/06jun20041800/
edocket.access.gpo.gov/2004/04-14170.htm

Afterschool.gov Finding Federal Dollars

http://www.afterschool.gov/feddollar1.html

This database sponsored by AfterSchool.Gov, part of the National Partnership for Reinventing Government, gives you one stop for information about more than 100 sources of federal funding for after-school and youth development programming.

American Academy of Pediatrics in the Real World Research Grants

http://www.aap.org/advocacy/learnrealworldrfp.pdf

The American Academy of Pediatrics (http://www.aap.org/) and Learning in the Real World (http://www.realworld.org/), a nonprofit organization interested in the use of education technology by K-12 students and preschool children, will fund year-long research grants that investigate questions relating to computer use and gross motor and visual motor development in young children. Infants and children up to the age of eleven are of particular interest. The maximum grant awarded is $50,000 per year.

American Legion Child Welfare Foundation

http://www.cwf-inc.org/

The American Legion Child Welfare Foundation was created to contribute to the physical, mental, emotional, and spiritual welfare of children and youth. The foundation makes grants that satisfy its basic purposes through the following mechanisms: (1) dissemination of knowledge about new and innovative organizations or their programs designed to benefit youth; and (2) dissemination of knowledge already possessed by well established organizations, so that this knowledge can be more adequately used by society. Grants are made for proposals that have the potential to directly benefit children in the United States in a large geographical area (more than one state). The duration is one year.

AT&T CARES Youth Service Action Fund

http://www.ysa.org/pdffiles/2003ATTC.pdf

Youth Service America and AT&T are proud to present the AT&T CARES Youth Service Action Fund to help young people engage in community service on National Youth Service Day and beyond. Fifty grants of $500 will be available to youth and organizations.

Best Buy Community Relations Grants Program

http://www.bestbuy.com/

The Best Buy Children's Foundation dedicates its resources in two primary ways: supporting the development and delivery of innovative, technology-based educational curriculum and content, and making education accessible to graduating high school seniors through Best Buy Scholarships. Our idea is simple: we want to make learning fun.

Binda Foundation (Guido and Elizabeth)
http://www.oaisd.org/tools/grant/grantS.htm?req=82
Provides grants of up to $200,000 to support substance abuse services, especially those connected to education and serving the economically disadvantaged and minority populations.

Blockbuster Community Relations
http://www.blockbuster.com/bb/about/bbcommunityrelations/0,7701,NT-ABT,00.html
Blockbuster sponsors several programs that use movies both to teach and reward students in schools across the U.S. More than 11,000 elementary schools are also taking part in our Blockbuster Class Act Award program, which allows elementary school teachers to reward their students' efforts with free movie rentals from BLOCKBUSTER.

Brookdale Foundation Group: Relatives as Parents Program
http://www.brookdalefoundation.org/rapp1.html
The Brookdale Relatives as Parents Program supports programs that develop or expand services for grandparents or other relatives that have taken on the responsibility of parenting when the biological parents are unwilling or unable to do so. Through the Local Initiative, the Foundation selects up to 15 local programs from within the United States to receive matching mini-grants of $10,000 over a two-year period.

Brooks Teammates for Kids Foundation (Garth)
http://www.touchemall.com/
http://www.teammatesforkids.org/index.htm
The Teammates for Kids Foundation accepts proposals for grants from nonprofit organizations that specialize in working with children. Grants from the Foundation support the on-going work of operating organizations that help needy children in the areas of health, education and inner-city services. While there are no minimum or maximum amounts, most grants range from $10,000 to $50,000. The Foundation's giving cycle is semi-annual.

Casey Foundation (Annie E.)
http://www.aecf.org

The Annie E. Casey Foundation considers support for public education and disadvantaged children one of its priorities. It is primarily interested in "initiatives that have significant potential to demonstrate innovative policy, service delivery, and community supports for children and families." Collaborative projects that engage parents in school improvement and the academic success of their children are within the foundation's area of interest. There are no deadlines. The first step in the grant-seeking process is to send the foundation a 2-3 page letter summarizing the proposed project, its goals, a brief history/background of the school, the population to be served, and the amount requested. If the foundation sees potential in the project, it will invite you to write a full proposal. The address: The Annie E. Casey Foundation, Attention: Office of the President, 701 St. Paul Street, Baltimore, MD 21202. Grant guidelines are also available at the foundation Web site, or from External Resources and Partnerships (ERP) by calling 773/553-2610, or e-mail at: erp@cps.k12.il.us.

Christian Children's Fund
http://www.christianchildrensfund.org/
For over 60 years CCF has been dedicated to providing assistance to needy children worldwide. Services are provided to approximately 2.5 million children regardless of race, religion, or gender in 31 countries, including the United States.

Community Toolbox for Children's Environmental Health
http://www.communitytoolbox.org/
The Community Toolbox for Children's Environmental Health provides small grants in conjunction with capacity building training and technical assistance to community-based environmental health and justice groups serving children in disproportionately impacted communities. Grants are provided to nonprofit organizations throughout the U.S. for programmatic and organizational capacity building activities in two areas: reducing environmental hazards that threaten the health of children and preventing childhood lead poisoning.

Daycare Grants and Child Care Grant and Funding Sources in the United States
http://www.childcare.net/grantsusa.shtml

Daycare Provider's Beginner Page: Funding Tips
http://www.oursite.net/daycare/grants.htm
Discusses "Are their grants for family daycare providers?"

Drug-Free Communities Support Program Funds Now Available
http://ojjdp.ncjrs.org/dfcs/
OJJDP and ONDCP announce the availability of Drug-Free Communities
Support Program funding. Approximately 180 grants of up to $100,000 each will
be awarded to community coalitions working to prevent youth substance abuse.
(OJJDP)

Duke Charitable Foundation (Doris)
http://www.ddcf.org
This foundation strives to improve the quality of people's lives by preserving natural environments, seeking cures for diseases, nurturing the arts, and helping to
protect children from abuse and neglect. The Foundation welcomes two-page letters of inquiry from nonprofit organizations working in the Foundation's areas of
interest. There is no deadline for letters of inquiry. For more information, call
Joan Spero at 212-974-7000.

Ebay Foundation
http://www.ebay.com/aboutebay/foundation/
The eBay Foundation makes grants to 501©(3) organizations for specific programs or projects that accomplish the following objectives: leverage existing
resources, foster collaboration, make a significant positive, long-term impact on
the people served.

Federov Foundation (Sergei)
http://www.sergeifedorov.com/foundation/scholarship1.htm
The Sergei Fedorov Foundation would give money to a variety of causes, including forming a partnership with Orchards Children's Services. One goal of the two
groups was to establish a specialized day camp for autistic and developmentally
disabled children. Another goal was to give scholarships for students from at-risk
backgrounds to attend Michigan universities. In addition to financial support,
the student will be placed in "a supportive and ongoing structure," including
summer employment, support groups, interaction with other Fedorov Scholars
and career counseling.

Finish Line Youth Foundation
Youth Athletic and Wellness Programs Supported
http://www.finishline.com/store/corporate_info/youthfoundation.jsp
The Finish Line Youth Foundation provides funding to organizations in the communities in which company stores are located, or communities where donations
to the Foundation are raised. The Foundation supports nonprofit organizations

primarily focused on assisting children and young adults 18 and under in the areas of athletics or wellness. Applications are accepted year-round and are reviewed quarterly.

Foundation for Child Development
http://www.ffcd.org/
A national private philanthropy dedicated to the principle that all families should have the social and material resources to raise their children to be healthy, educated, and productive members of their communities.

FreddieMac Foundation
http://www.freddiemacfoundation.org/core/grants/
Will continue to support programs that focus on the important work of preventing child abuse and neglect and finding permanent homes for children in foster care. In the future, we will expand our historical support of children and their families during the early stages of a child's life to include children from birth to 18 years of age. In addition to supporting youth as they transition to adulthood, a special emphasis will be placed on programs that help young people aging out of foster care obtain stable housing and successfully move to independence.

Funding for after school
http://www.afterschool.org/funding.cfm
Courtesy of Promising Practices in After school.

Funding Opportunities for Child Care
http://www.nccic.org/faqs/funding.html
Advice from the National Child Care Information Center.

Georgia Master Gardener Grant List
http://www.ces.uga.edu/Agriculture/horticulture/Master%20Gardener/grantlist.html
Sources of funding for starting a children's garden.

Gerber Foundation
http://www.gerberfoundation.org/
To enhance the quality of life of infants and young children in nutrition, care, and development.

Good Neighbor Service-Learning Award
http://www.ysa.org/pdffiles/2003_GN.pdf

(Deadline—February
The State Farm Good Neighbor Service-Learning Award enables youth and educators to bring positive benefits of service-learning to more young people. This grant is for both young people ages 5-25 and teachers to implement service-learning projects for National Youth Service Day 2003, April 11-13th. Fifty grants of $500 each will be available to young people and fifty grants of $1,500 will be available to teachers (to engage classes).

Grantmakers for Children, Youth, and Families
http://www.gcyf.org/
A web page of potential interest.

Handspring Foundation
http://www.handspring.com/company/foundation/
The Handspring Foundation makes cash grants and product donations to non-profit organizations and overseas equivalents that focus on pre-K-12 education or issues directly related to children/youth at risk. Particularly attractive to the foundation are programs that use the arts, technology, or sports to help high-risk youth, provide direct child-health services, and assist youth who are victims of abuse and neglect or are homeless.

Hasbro Children's Foundation
http://www.hasbro.org
The mission of the Foundation is to improve the quality of life for disadvantaged children through age 12 by supporting innovative, model, direct-service programs in the areas of health education and social services. The Foundation also funds universally accessible play spaces. Most often, local grants for model community programs range from $500 to $35,000 each. For multi-site expansions, awards start at $35,000 and are granted over a period of one to three years. Priority will be given to economically disadvantaged areas for playground refurbishment and/or new construction. For more information, contact Hasbro Children's Foundation, 32 W. 23rd St., New York, NY 10010. Proposals are reviewed three times per year; there is no deadline for applications. For more information contact: Jane S. Englebardt, 917-606-6226.

Hasbro Children's Foundation
A Strong Commitment to Children
http://www.hasbro.org/hcf/
The Hasbro Children's Foundation is committed to improving the emotional, mental and physical well-being of children up to the age of twelve and their families

through the support of innovative direct service programs in the areas of health, education and social services. The Foundation's funding helps to provide the support children need to grow up healthy and strong, to bring innovative programs to children throughout the nation, and to resolve the issues that put children at risk in the first place. There is no deadline for applications; requests are reviewed three times a year. Visit the website above for complete application information.

Head Start
http://www.acf.dhhs.gov/programs/hsb
Provides early, continuous, intensive and comprehensive child development and family support services on a year-round basis to low-income families. The purpose of the Early Head Start program is to enhance children's physical, social, emotional, and intellectual development; to support parents' efforts to fulfill their parental roles; and, to help parents move toward self-sufficiency.

Help Us Help Foundation
http://www.helpushelp.org
With financial support provided by database software giant Oracle Corporation, the nonprofit Help Us Help Foundation assists K-12 public schools and youth organizations in economically challenged communities to obtain information technology tools. Grants of computer equipment and software are available to schools and youth organizations in the U.S. that provide educational programs in low-income communities.

Home Depot Corporation
http://www.HomeDepot.com/

Houston Foundation for Children (Whitney)
http://www.whfoundation.com/

International Youth Foundation
http://www.iyfnet.org/
Currently operating in nearly 50 countries and territories, the International Youth Foundation (IYF) is one of the world's largest public foundations working to improve the conditions and prospects for young people where they live, learn, work, and play.

JC Penny Afterschool Grant Program
http://jcpenneyafterschool.org/

JCPenney Afterschool is a $30 million, multi-year program designed to expand curriculum-based after school programs. JC Penny has targeted pre-kindergarten through grade 12 education as a focus for its corporate giving and associate involvement, particularly dropout prevention and school reform and restructuring efforts. Proposals are accepted year-round. Minor grants of less than $5,000 are made year-round. Major grants of $5,000 or more are made following quarterly meetings of the J.C. Penney's Public Affairs Committee.

Join Hands Day
Youth Excellence Awards
http://www.joinhandsday.org/scripts/awards_excellence_index.cfm
Twenty awardees are selected from thousands of volunteer projects that develop youth and adult partnerships on Join Hands Day. Each winning project receives a $1,000 check and an engraved glass award. Coordinating groups choose how the funds are used. Some organizations find it appropriate to donate the money to the beneficiary of the project or another benevolent cause. Others choose to save it as seed money for next year's event.

KidsGardening.Com : Healthy Sprouts Award
http://www.kidsgardening.com/grants.asp#sprouts
The National Gardening Association and Gardener's Supply Company have partnered to support schools and community organizations that use gardens to teach about nutrition and explore the issue of hunger in the United States. Each of twenty-five programs receives an award package of seeds, tools, garden products, and educational resources for growing a vegetable garden. Five of these programs also receive $500 cash and a $200 gift certificate to the Gardener's Supply Company catalog.

KidsGardening.Com : "Room to Grow" Juliana Greenhouse Grant
http://www.kidsgardening.com/grants.asp#greenhouse
The National Gardening Association has partnered with Juliana, manufacturers of hobby greenhouses to create the "Room to Grow" Juliana Greenhouse Grant. Schools and community organizations across the U.S. with established youth gardens are invited to apply. Applicants must involve at least 15 youngsters between the ages of 3 and 18 in gardening in 2004. 50 selected projects will receive indoor growing equipment and/or materials. Prizes range from a large Professional Horticultural Greenhouse (retail value $2,495) to NGA's Guide to School Greenhouses.

Kmart Community Outreach Programs
http://www.kmartcorp.com/corp/community/index.stm

Look under the "About KMart Section" for information about community outreach programs. Check out the KMart Fund for Kids.

Kohl's Fundraising Card Program
http://www.kohlscorporation.com/CommunityRelations/Community04.htm
The Kohl's Cares for Kids® Fundraising Card Program benefits school and nonprofit youth organizations through the use of special gift cards. The fundraising card is an electronic gift card sold to school organizations and youth groups at a discount of 5% for total gift card purchases over $1000 and 3% for purchases from $500 to $999. The fundraising groups then sell the purchased cards at face value and keep the profits.

Lesko's Help for Kids and Pets
http://www.lesko.com/help/HelpForKidsandPets.htm
Money, information and services for the care and feeding of kids and pets.

Lets Just Play Grant Program
http://www.nick.com/all_nick/everything_nick/public_ljpgrants2.jhtml
The "Lets Just Play" campaign by Nickelodeon will award a half-million dollars in grants to schools and after-school programs to provide resources to create and expand opportunities for physical play. Elementary schools, middle schools and after-school programs across the country are eligible to enter the grants program.

Magic Johnson Foundation
http://magicjohnson.org/
Dedicated to serving the educational, health, and social needs of minority youth and underserved communities throughout the nation.

Mailman Family Foundation (A.W.)
http://www.mailman.org/
Funding nonprofit and academic proposals which support programs for children and families, with special emphasis on early childhood. Also provides links to additional funders.

Make a Wish Foundation of Michigan
http://www.wishmich.org/
This organization does its best to make dreams come true for children with terminal illnesses.

McKenzie Foundation
http://www.mckenziefoundation.us/guidelines.php

Mervyn's Community Giving
http://target.com/mervyns_group/community/community_main.jhtml
A Friend is Also a Good Neighbor. That's why Mervyn's adopted the phrase "You've Got a Friend in Mervyn's" for our community giving program. We extend a hand of friendship through financial support, volunteer activities, and involvement in local nonprofit initiatives. It's our goal to help thousands of children and families across the country, and make many new friends along the way. Because Mervyn's store managers know their communities best, Mervyn's grant programs start and end with them. If you are involved with a nonprofit program you believe would benefit from a grant, get more information and learn how to apply. Most grants average between $500 and $2,500. Mervyn's also sponsors a Local Hero scholarship program for students graduating from high school who wish to attend college or vocational schools.

Michigan Community Service Commission
Funding Opportunities
http://www.michigan.gov/mcsc/1,1607,7-137-6114—-,00.html
Annually, the MCSC grants approximately $7.5 million in federal funds and $780,000 in state funds to nonprofit organizations, schools, and other agencies to support National Service and volunteer activities in Michigan.

Michigan State University
Institute for Children, Youth, and Families
Federal Funding Opportunities
http://www.icyf.msu.edu/funding/fedfund.html

MIChild
http://www.michigan.gov/mdch/1,1607,7-132-2943_4845_4931—-,00.html
MIChild is a health insurance program. It is for uninsured children of Michigan's working families. MIChild services are provided by many HMOs and other health care plans throughout Michigan. For more information, call your health plan, the local Family Independence Agency, your local health department or call 1-888-988-6300.

Milagro Foundation
http://www.santana.com/frameset2.html

Foundation created by Carlos Santana to provide funding to grass roots organizations serving children and youth.

National 4-H Council Youth Grant Programs
http://www.fourhcouncil.edu/programs/index.asp
The Youth-Corporate Connections team of National 4-H Council offers grants for youth in local communities, in counties, and on the state level. These grants provide opportunities for young people and adults to take action on issues critical to their lives, their families, and their communities. Note: no grants to individuals, just organizations.

National Adoption Foundation
http://www.nafadopt.org/NAFPrograms.htm
The National Adoption Foundation helps arrange loans and provides limited grants for parents to cover expenses before and after adoption. They also provide information on sources of other financial help like the 325 Fortune 500 companies who offer an average cash reimbursement of $4,000 for their employees who adopt, or the new adoption expense tax credit that is available from the IRS. Contact: National Adoption Foundation, 100 Mill Plain Rd, Danbury, CT 06811; Telephone: 203-791-3811.

National Clearinghouse on Child Abuse and Neglect Information Funding Sources
http://web.archive.org/web/20030604120313/
http://calib.com/nccanch/funding/index.cfm
Across the nation, community-based organizations, public and non-profit agencies, universities, service providers, trainers, and researchers are working to help protect children. An array of potential funding sources is available to support these efforts, including Federal and State agencies, foundations, and private corporations. Still available thanks to the Internet Archive.

National Youth Development Information Center Guide to Government Funds
http://www.nydic.org/nydic/funding/government/index.htm
The federal government funds a number of youth programs. While most are not "strictly" youth development programs, many offer local agencies the opportunity to provide youth-related services within a youth development approach.

Newman's Own Charitable Foundation
http://www.newmansown.com/

Offers grants to nonprofits, schools, hospitals, and other 501(c)(3) public benefit organizations. Eligible grant categories include: the arts, children and youth, health, education, the elderly, environment, the handicapped, literacy, substance abuse education, programs for the needy including housing and food, but no funding for individuals or scholarships.

Office Depot: Caring and Making a Difference
http://www.community.officedepot.com/local.asp
Office Depot supports nonprofit organizations at the local level with donations of products, contributions of funds and efforts to encourage employees and customers to become involved.

Perpetual Preschool Fundraising Ideas
http://www.perpetualpreschool.com/fundideas.html

Public Welfare Foundation Youth Grants
http://www.publicwelfare.org/grants/disadvantaged_youth.asp
Approximately $2 million is available to address:

☐ Employment, Training and Alternative Education—Programs that provide quality education, employment readiness services with job placement and other assistance for young people who have dropped out of school, experience chronic unemployment, and have minimal or no job skills, so that they may achieve independent living for themselves and their families.
☐ Early Intervention—Programs that promote positive youth development through services designed to prevent educational failure, delinquency, developmental delays, adverse health, or neglect. Services also include assistance to children whose parents are adolescents, affected by HIV/AIDS, involved in substance abuse, or incarcerated.
☐ Youth Leadership Development—Programs that provide opportunities for youth leadership development in conjunction with efforts to address problems facing young people and their communities.
☐ Violence Prevention—Primary prevention services to reduce violence in neighborhoods and families, especially violence caused by the availability of guns and other weapons.
☐ Advocacy and Policy Development—Programs that promote systemic responsiveness to the needs of low-income young people within federal, state and local policies and practices>

Radio Shack Corp
Neighborhood Answers Program
http://www.radioshackcorporation.com/
Radio Shack Corp, the Fort Worth, Texas-based consumer electronics retailer, is accepting applications for its new Neighborhood Answers Grant Program. This program is designed to fund worthy causes that help families protect children from abduction, violence and abuse. Grants are limited to $500 or less.

Ronald McDonald House Charities
http://www.rmhc.com/grant/index.html
Ronald McDonald House Charities provides grants to not-for-profit, tax exempt organizations whose national or global programs help children reach their fullest potential.

Rural Assistance Center
Child Care Funding
http://www.raconline.org/info_guides/child_care/index.php

Rural Information Center
Rural Child Care Funding and Program Resources
http://www.nal.usda.gov/ric/faqs/childc-1.htm#funding

Save the Children
http://www.savethechildren.org/
Provide services in 18 states across the United States and in 46 developing nations around the world.

Staples Foundation for Learning
http://www.staplesfoundation.org/foundapplication.html
The mission of Staples Foundation for Learning is to provide funding to programs that support or provide job skills and/or education for all people, with a special emphasis on disadvantaged youth.

Thomas Foundation for Adoption (Dave)
http://www.davethomasfoundationforadoption.org/
The Dave Thomas Foundation for Adoption's primary interest is in funding projects that directly impact permanency through adoption of waiting children in the United States and Canada. The Foundation is especially interested in addressing the permanency needs of children who are older, who have medical or emotional

difficulties; children who are from an ethnic minority and sibling groups of children seeking adoption together.

Touch'Em All Foundation
http://members.aol.com/Nutts4GB/TEAF.html
The Touch'em All Foundation accepts proposals for grants from nonprofit organizations that specialize in working with children. Grants from the Foundation support the on-going work of operating organizations that help needy children in the areas of health, education and the inner-city services. The Foundation's giving cycle is semi-annual. Funded by Garth Brooks.

Traina Foundation (Nick)
http://www.nicktrainafoundation.org/main.htm
The Nick Traina Foundation was founded in 1998 by best-selling author Danielle Steel as a legacy to her son who lost his life to manic-depression. The Foundation supports organizations involved in the diagnosis, research, treatment, and/or family support of manic-depression, suicide prevention, child abuse and children in jeopardy. Assistance is also provided to struggling musicians in the areas of health and mental illness.

Trust Fund for Children With Special Needs
http://www.mdch.state.mi.us/msa/cshcs/
For more than 50 years, the Trust Fund for Children with Special Health Care Needs has been located in the Children's Special Health Care Services program (formerly known as the Crippled Children's Program) and has been a resource for Michigan families of children with special health care needs.

WalMart Foundation
http://www.walmartfoundation.org/
Through its community involvement program, WalMart provides funding to a number of nonprofits working in the areas of children, community, education, and environment. WalMart also provides scholarships to associates.

Whirlpool Foundation
http://www.whirlpoolcorp.com/social_responsibility/default.asp
Seek to improve the quality of life in our home communities, such as Benton Harbor, worldwide. We particularly like to be partners with organizations that target the social issues of lifelong learning, cultural diversity and contemporary family life.

Youth in Action Grants
http://www.youthlink.org/us/
Grants of $1000 are available for projects that fulfill community needs and create positive impact.

Youth Related Foundations
http://www.cdsfunds.com/youth-related_foundations.html

Youth Service America
Awards and Grants
http://www.ysa.org/awards/award_grant.cfm
Describes:

☐ Youth Leaders for Literacy Grants
☐ Harris Wofford Awards

Youth Service America: The State Farm Good Neighbor Service-Learning Award
http://www.ysa.org/awards/award_grant.cfm
The State Farm Good Neighbor Service-Learning Award, sponsored by the State Farm Companies Foundation and administered by Youth Service America, enables youth and educators to bring positive benefits of service-learning to more young people.

Youth Services Grants Available from the U.S. Government
http://www.cfda.gov/public/grantsubtopic.asp?catcode=N#JMP19
Courtesy of the Catalog of Federal Domestic Assistance

GRANTS FOR NONPROFITS

Religion and Social Change

ActivistCash.com Foundation Directory
http://www.activistcash.com/index_foundations.cfm
In addition to providing a directory of foundations that have funded activist organizations, this web page also provides a directory of activist groups, celebrities who support activist organizations, and key players.

Ben & Jerry's Foundation Grants for Social Change
http://www.benjerry.com/foundation/index.html
Ben & Jerry's Foundation, endowed by the makers of Cherry Garcia and Chocolate Chip Cookie Dough ice creams, offers grants of $1,001 to $15,000 for programs working for social, institutional, or environmental change. The foundation generally sponsors 501(c)(3) or fiscally sponsored nonprofit organizations with budgets under $250,000 per year.

Bonner Foundation (Corella & Bertram F.)
http://www.bonner.org,br> The Corella and Bertram F. Bonner Foundation will consider providing support to:

▢ Community-based crisis ministry programs that are sponsored by a congregation or a coalition of congregations, which show a strong initiative in leadership in the fight against hunger and related issues in their community.
▢ Develop innovative nutritious food programs and special projects through food banks, SHAREs and other regional support networks to fight hunger and address its underlying issues.

(Jimmy) Buffet's Singing for Change (SFC) Charitable Foundation
http://margaritaville.com/sfc/

SFC is interested in funding projects that improve the quality of life for people and that empower individuals to effect positive change in their communities. Most likely to be considered are organizations that keep their overhead low and collaborate with other groups in their community to find innovative ways of solving common problems. Grants awarded usually fall in the $500 to $10,000 range.

Calvin Institute of Christian Worship
Worship Renewal Grants Program
http://www.calvin.edu/worship/wrgp/index.htm
Designed to foster well-grounded worship renewal in congregations throughout North America. Made possible through the generous support of Lilly Endowment Inc., these grants are intended to serve a grass-roots constituency of those concerned for the vitality of the worship life in their local Christian communities in a variety of denominations. Through its grantmaking, the Calvin Institute of Christian Worship intends to stimulate thoughtful and energetic work that will result in worship services that exhibit renewed creativity, theological integrity, and relevance.

Catholic Campaign for Human Development Grants
http://www.usccb.org/cchd/grant.htm
CCHD is committed to supporting groups of low-income individuals as they work to break the cycle of poverty and improve their communities. By helping the poor to participate in the decisions and actions that affect their lives, CCHD empowers them to move beyond poverty. CCHD funds two categories of projects: organizing and economic development.

Catholic Charities USA
http://www.catholiccharitiesusa.org/
Supporting families, reducing poverty, and building communities. Follow the links to find local offices in each state.

Center for Faith-Based and Community Initiatives
http://www.hhs.gov/faith
The U.S. Department of Health and Human Services sponsors this page in an effort to provide a central information resource for programs and opportunities for faith-based and community organizations. The site features a compilation of HHS funding opportunities listed by topic and program office, with guidance on how organizations should apply.

Church Women United
http://www.churchwomen.org/
Through Intercontinental Grants For Mission, CWU funds global and domestic microeconomic projects that develop and empower women or are led by women. Projects are judged by committee (application deadline is August 1) and grants range from $250-$5000.

Coon (Joanne Cross) Foundation
http://www.lib.msu.edu/harris23/grants/privloc.htm#coon
Provides grants to Seventh Day Adventist organizations and activities.

Evangelical Lutheran Church in America
Domestic Hunger Program
http://www.elca.org/grantinghope/
The Evangelical Lutheran Church in America Domestic Hunger Program provides assistance to fight hunger throughout the United States. Support is provided for relief, with a focus on access to food, shelter, clothing, medical supplies and care to meet basic human needs; sustainable development; community organizing; and education and advocacy efforts addressing the causes and elimination of hunger and poverty. Priority will be given to projects that focus on meeting the basic needs of the people with the least resources and women and children living in poverty.

Faith-Based Centers and Community Initiatives
http://www.whitehouse.gov/government/fbci/grants-catalog-index.html
http://www.nal.usda.gov/ric/faqs/volfaq.htm#faith
Discusses federal funding and grant programs available to faith-based organizations.

Fund for Nonviolence
http://www.fundfornonviolence.org/
The Fund for Nonviolence cultivates and supports community based efforts to bring about social change that moves humanity towards a more just and compassionate coexistence.

Gilmore Foundation (Mertz)
http://www.mertzgilmore.org/www/default_flash.html
The Mertz Gilmore Foundation's new human rights program works to advance human rights in the U.S. Support is provided for projects that demonstrate what and how human rights can contribute to social justice in the U.S.; networks and coalitions that build and strengthen cross-issue and/or cross-constituency linkages;

and capacity building through human rights training. Projects will be considered across the full spectrum of human rights—economic, social and cultural as well as civil and political—and support a variety of constituencies, and/or methods. Nonprofit organizations and coalitions or networks of organizations throughout the United States are eligible to apply. Letters of inquiry are accepted throughout the year.

Hebrew Free Loan Association
http://www.hflasf.org/fund-source.html

Jewish Federation of Metropolitan Detroit
http://www.jfmd.org/
In partnership with its agencies, Federation plays the leadership role in identifying needs within the Jewish community and in mobilizing human and financial resources, engaging in communal planning and allocation and advocating to meet those needs.

Johnson (Robert Wood) Faith in Action Program
http://www.fiavolunteers.org/
Faith in Action is a national volunteer movement that brings together religious congregations from many faiths and other community organizations. Their common mission is to help people who are aging and chronically ill maintain their independence by providing them assistance with everyday activities. The program will be giving $35,000 grants to 2,000 organizations in the next six years, plus technical assistance. They're looking for organizations that have five things: they're interfaith, they use volunteers, they provide caregiving services, to people with chronic health conditions, and the services are provided in people's homes. It's a $100 million program, one of the ten largest foundation grants ever, according to USA Today.

Lutheran Social Services of Michigan
http://www.lssm.org/
A service-organization of the Evangelical Lutheran Church of America.

Mustard Seed Foundation
http://www.msfdn.org/home/index.cfm
Inspired by the parable of the mustard seed found in Mark 4 and Matthew 13, we seek to be stewards by participating in the expansion and realization of the kingdom of God on earth. We do this by providing grants to churches and Christian

organizations worldwide as they initiate a variety of Christian ministries including evangelism, discipleship, and economic empowerment.

Muste (A. J.) Memorial Institute
http://www.nonviolence.org/ajmuste/
Projects with small budgets…and little chance of funding from more traditional sources are supported by the A.J. Muste Memorial Institute. The Institute funds projects that promote the principles and practice of nonviolent social change. About 20 to 30 grants are made annually. For more information contact Murray Rosenblith by phone or email, 212-533-4335, ajmusteinst@igc.org.

National Benevolent Association of the Christian Church (Disciples of Christ)
http://WWW.NBACARES.ORG/

North American Mission Board
Church Finance Ministry
http://www.namb.net/root/churchfinance/
For over 100 years, we have assisted local Southern Baptist churches in obtaining financing for their building needs. We offer both consultation services and loans to qualified Southern Baptist churches. Our consultation is freely given as a means to assist your church as you plan for its financial future. Our lending programs may be used for purchasing properties, refinance of existing debt, as well as for construction and renovation projects.

Presbyterian Committee on the Self-Development of People
http://www.pcusa.org/sdop/theological.htm
The Presbyterian Committee on the Self-Development of People supports grassroots projects that are developed, owned, and controlled by groups of poor, oppressed, and disadvantaged people. Priority is given to local projects rather than regional, statewide, or national projects. Generally, annual grants range from $10,000 to $50,000 for projects in the U.S.

Religious Foundations
http://www.cdsfunds.com/religious_foundations.html
A list of web links provided by Custom Development Solutions, Inc., a consulting firm located in Isle of Palms, S.C.

Rubin Foundation (Samuel)
http://www.samuelrubinfoundation.org/

The Samuel Rubin Foundation is dedicated to the pursuit of peace and justice and the search for an equitable reallocation of the world's resources. Grants are awarded to support projects that address the issues of implementation of social, economic, political, civil, and cultural rights for all the world's people.

Rural Assistance Center
Faith-Based Initiatives Funding
http://www.raconline.org/info_guides/faith/

Salvation Army
http://www.salvationarmy.org/
Provide emergency relief both domestic and worldwide.

Save the Children
http://www.savethechildren.org/
Provide services in 18 states across the United States and in 46 developing nations around the world.

Thrivent Financial for Lutherans Foundation
E-mail: mail@thrivent.com
Provides loans for new churches, schools and church buildings; renovations and remodeling For more information, contact: Church Loan Staff, Thrivent Financial for Lutherans, 4321 North Ballard Road, Appleton, Wisconsin 54919-0001; Telephone: 800) 847-4836, extension 85701.

Top 50 Foundations Awarding Grants in Religion, 1999
http://fdncenter.org/fc_stats/subject01_99.html
Courtesy of the Foundation Center.

Top 50 U.S. Foundations Awarding Grants in Religion
http://fdncenter.org/fc_stats/pdf/04_fund_sub/2001/50_found_sub/f_sub_x_01.pdf
Source: FC Stats.

United Jewish Communities
http://www.ujc.org/
The merger of the United Jewish Appeal, Council of Jewish Federations, and United Israel Appeal has created a new national organization dedicated to seizing this opportunity to improve people's lives—around the corner and around the globe. Take a look at the Local Links for local affiliates.

Whitely (John and Elizabeth) Foundation
http://www.lib.msu.edu/harris23/grants/privloc.htm#whiteley
Support Episcopal churches and seminaries in Ingham County.

Widow's Mite Foundation
http://www.pastorsnet.com/caregiver_ministries/members/widows_mite_found.html
The Widow's Mite Foundation is a non profit 501c tax deductible private foundation designed to financially support high impact, doctrinally sound, Christian ministries though counseling, mentoring, training, consulting, nurturing, and furnishing.

Women of the ECLA Grants Programs
http://www.womenoftheelca.org/whatwedo/grants.html
Ministries throughout the United States and the international community will continue to strengthen families and communities with the help of grants awarded by Women of the ELCA. The women's organization has awarded more than $2.5 million in grants since 1988 to support ministries that see people and communities as assets rather than objects of need.

GRANTS FOR NONPROFITS

COMMUNITY DEVELOPMENT

Bank of America Corporation
http://www.bankofamerica.com/community/
Bank of America is recognized as a national leader in the community development industry. This leadership role is based on results that have helped bring positive change to communities through the development of affordable housing, the financing of small businesses and the identification of new ways in which Bank of America can use creativity, partnerships and expertise to help communities thrive.

Catholic Campaign for Human Development Grants
http://www.usccb.org/cchd/grant.htm
CCHD is committed to supporting groups of low-income individuals as they work to break the cycle of poverty and improve their communities. By helping the poor to participate in the decisions and actions that affect their lives, CCHD empowers them to move beyond poverty. CCHD funds two categories of projects: organizing and economic development.

Community Development Grants from the U.S. Government
Posted on the Catalog of Federal Domestic Assistance
http://www.cfda.gov/public/grantsubtopic.asp?catcode=C
Subcategories include: Planning and Research, Construction, Renewal, and Operations, Historical Preservation, Rural Community Development, Recreation, Site Acquisition, Indian Action Services, Federal Surplus Property, Technical Assistance and Services, Land Acquistion, and Fire Protection.

Community Development Grants from the U.S. Government
Posted on Grants.gov
http://www.grants.gov/FindGrantOpportunities
Some of the most current grant opportunities posted by the federal government.

Community Development Toolbox
http://www.ezec.gov/toolbox/index.html
A collection of resources available over the web dealing with community development. Sponsored by the Empowerment Zone and Enterprise Community Program of the U.S. Department of Housing and Urban Development.

Community Improvement/Development Funding Opportunities Posted by the Foundation Center RFP Bulletin
http://fdncenter.org/pnd/rfp/cat_community.jhtml

Cooperative Development Foundation
http://www.cdf.coop/
The Cooperative Development Foundation promotes self-help and mutual aid in community, economic, and social development through cooperative enterprise. CDF works to bring together the funds and partners to incubate and replicate cooperative solutions to people's needs. CDF administers a number of funds supporting cooperative activities ranging from helping people move from welfare to work, creating affordable housing co-ops for rural seniors, and creating value-added agriculture co-ops to help farmers increase their market share.

Economic Development Grant Programs from the U.S. Government
http://www.cfda.gov/public/browse_sub.asp?subcode=BL&st=1
A subset of the Catalog of Federal Domestic Assistance.

Enterprise MoneyNet
http://www.enterprisefoundation.org/resources/Funding/moneynet/index.asp
Enterprise MoneyNet™ helps you find public and private funding resources to support your organization and its programs. We review and add information daily to this growing database of more than 800 donors.

Federal Funding Opportunities for Community Development Posted on Grants.gov
http://www.grants.gov/FindGrantOpportunities
Lists some of the most recent grant programs available.

Federal Funding Opportunities for Regional Development Posted on Grants.gov
http://www.grants.gov/FindGrantOpportunities
Lists some of the most recent grant programs available.

Federal Funding Opportunities for Transportation Posted on Grants.gov
http://www.grants.gov/FindGrantOpportunities

Lists some of the most recent grant programs available. Note: Select transportation as funding activity category before initiating search.

Federal Funding Sources for Rural Areas, FY2003
http://www.nal.usda.gov/ric/ricpubs/funding/federalfund/ff.html
A collection of resources from the Catalog of Federal Domestic Assistance compiled by the Rural Information Center Program of the National Agricultural Library.

Ford Foundation
Asset Building and Community Development
http://www.fordfound.org/program/asset_main.cfm
The Asset Building and Community Development program helps strengthen and increase the effectiveness of people and organizations working to find solutions to problems of poverty and injustice.

Foundation Center RFP Bulletin : Community Development/Improvement
http://fdncenter.org/pnd/rfp/cat_community.jhtml
The RFP (Request for Proposals) Bulletin is published weekly by the Foundation Center. Each RFP listing provides a brief overview of a current funding opportunity offered by a foundation or other grantmaking organization.

Foundations for Community-Based Efforts
http://www.cdsfunds.com/foundations_for_community-based_efforts.html
A list of web links provided by Custom Development Solutions, Inc.

Grants.gov: Current Federal Funding Opportunities for Community Development
http://www.grants.gov/FindGrantOpportunities

Grants.gov: Current Federal Funding Opportunities for Regional Development
http://www.grants.gov/FindGrantOpportunities

Grants.gov : Current Federal Funding Opportunities for Transportation
http://www.grants.gov/FindGrantOpportunities

Hewlett Packard Microenterprize Development Program
http://h21030.www2.hp.com/us/programs/micro_index.html
The goal of the program is to make microenterprise-development agencies more effective and assist them in providing their clients with access to technology and associated training. Each grant award has a total list price value of $150,000 to

$300,000 in equipment, cash, services and support. In addition, recipients receive a travel grant to participate in a symposium focused on increasing the capacity of the microenterprise development industry.

Land Acquistion Grants/Programs of the U.S. Government
http://www.cfda.gov/public/grantsubtopic.asp?catcode=C#JMP10

Leadership for a Changing World
http://www.leadershipforchange.org/
The Ford Foundation is seeking nominations of community leaders across the country who are successfully tackling tough social problems for the Leadership for a Changing World program. Twenty outstanding social justice leaders and leadership teams that are not broadly known beyond their immediate community or field will receive awards of $100,000 to advance their work, plus $30,000 for supporting activities.

Local Initiatives Support Corporation (LISC)
http://www.liscnet.org/whatwedo/facts/
Local Initiatives Support Corporation (LISC) was founded in 1979 and is the nation's largest community building organization. LISC's mission is to rebuild whole communities by supporting Community Development Corporations (CDCs).

Michigan Cool City Catalyst Grants
http://www.michigan.gov/gov/0,1607,7-168-29544_29546_29555—-,00.html
The Granholm administration has kicked off a new program that includes grants up of to $100,000 to revitalize neighborhoods.

Presbyterian Committee on the Self-Development of People
http://www.pcusa.org/sdop/theological.htm
The Presbyterian Committee on the Self-Development of People supports grass-roots projects that are developed, owned, and controlled by groups of poor, oppressed, and disadvantaged people. Priority is given to local projects rather than regional, statewide, or national projects. Generally, annual grants range from $10,000 to $50,000 for projects in the U.S.

Public Welfare Foundation Community Development Grants
http://www.publicwelfare.org/grants/cedp.asp
$2.5 million is currently allocated to address:

◻ Grassroots or Local Organizations—Programs that are guided by and actively involve low-income people in addressing issues including homelessness, affordable housing and economic participation, and in providing direct service to low-income people in these and other issue areas. Particular interest in community organizing and leadership development and community and capacity building efforts.

◻ Low-wage Workers—Programs that strengthen and support organizing efforts among low-wage workers to improve working conditions, seek improved wages, and address broader economic issues.

◻ Technical Assistance to Grassroots or Local Organizations—Programs that enhance the effectiveness of organizations by providing technical assistance, training or analysis on issues affecting low-income communities.

◻ Advocacy and Policy Development—Advocacy and empowerment programs that promote local, state, national or international policies that reflect the needs of low-income communities.

Regional Development Grants from the U.S. Government
Posted on the Catalog of Federal Domestic Assistance
http://www.cfda.gov/public/grantsubtopic.asp?catcode=R
Subcategories include: Economic Development, Planning and Technical Assistance, Land Acquisition and Rehabilitation and Facilities Construction, Transportation, Energy, Housing, Education, Health and Nutrition, and Resources and Development.

Regional Development Grants/Programs from the U.S. Government
Posted on Grants.gov
http://www.grants.gov/FindGrantOpportunities
Some of the most current grant opportunities posted by the federal government.

Rural Assistance Center
Capital Funding Sources
http://www.raconline.org/info_guides/funding/capital.php
Rural Capital Assistance Funding is funding used to expand or renovate a building, purchase major equipment or construct a new facility for a rural health provider. Funding for capital expenditures usually needs to be secured from a variety of sources, both public and private.

Rural Assistance Center
Job Creation and Microenterprise Development Funding
http://www.raconline.org/info_guides/jobcreation/index.php

Rural Assistance Center
Job Retention and Career Advancement Funding
http://www.raconline.org/info_guides/jobretention/index.php

Rural Community Development Grants from the U.S. Government
http://www.cfda.gov/public/grantsubtopic.asp?catcode=C#JMP4

Seliger Funding Report: Community Development/Housing
http://www.seliger.com/GrantAlert/default.cfm
If you register with Seliger and Associates, a fundraising firm, they will allow you access to a sampler of possible funding opportunities and provide you with free e-mail updates.

Small Business and Self-Employment Service (SBSES)
State Economic Development Resources
http://www.jan.wvu.edu/SBSES/ECONOMICDEVELOPMENT.HTM
These listings represent a variety of state resources related to economic development, funding assistance, and growing a small or home-based business. It is worthwhile to spend some time on the website(s) for your state.

Smart Communities Network: Funding Opportunities
http://www.sustainable.doe.gov/management/financl.shtml

State Farm Foundation
http://www.statefarm.com/foundati/cogrants.htm
The State Farm Companies Foundation makes charitable contributions to non-profit, tax-exempt organizations under Section 501(c)(3) of the U.S. Internal Revenue Code, Canadian charitable organizations, and educational institutions. Proposals are accepted year-round and are reviewed in a timely manner. However, approval time depends on the requesting amount and completeness of the proposal. Requests exceeding $100,000 are considered quarterly.

Top 50 Foundations Awarding Grants for Community Improvement and Development, 1999
http://fdncenter.org/fc_stats/subject01_99.html

Top 50 U.S. Foundations Awarding Grants for Community Improvement and Development, 2001
http://fdncenter.org/fc_stats/pdf/04_fund_sub/2001/50_found_sub/f_sub_s_01.pdf

Trickle Up Organization
http://www.trickleup.org/
Founded in 1979, the Trickle Up Program's mission is to help the lowest income people worldwide take the first step up out of poverty, by providing conditional seed capital and business training essential to the launch of a microenterprise.

U.S. Department of Labor
Occupational Safety and Health Organization
Susan Harwood Training Grants Program
http://www.osha-slc.gov/fso/ote/training/sharwood/sharwood.html
OSHA awards grants on a competitive basis through its Susan Harwood Training Grant Program. Grants are awarded to nonprofit organizations to provide training and education programs or to develop training materials for employers and workers on the recognition, avoidance, and prevention of safety and health hazards in their workplaces.

WalMart Foundation
http://www.walmartfoundation.org/
Through its community involvement program, WalMart provides funding to a number of nonprofits working in the areas of children, community, education, and environment. WalMart also provides scholarships to associates.

GRANTS FOR NONPROFITS

EDUCATION

7-Eleven Community Outreach Programs
http://www.7-eleven.com/about/outreachprograms.asp
7-Eleven supports non-profits, libraries, and schools particularly in the following areas: (1) Education is our signature cause, specifically programs that assist adolescents and adults (ages 14 and above) with: Workforce Developmentand Language Education. 7-Eleven is especially interested in programs that assist at-risk and economically disadvantaged individuals. (2) The company also supports educational programs that recognize the rich cultural diversity in our communities and promote better understanding and tolerance among cultures throughout America. 7-Eleven has a specific interest in programs that serve ethnic and inner-city constituents. (3) 7-Eleven supports programs designed to prevent crime and build stronger, safer and more caring communities, with a special interest in youth-related programs. (4) 7-Eleven also supports the fight against hunger, providing by in-kind contributions of fresh foods to pre-selected food banks in markets where 7-Eleven operates.
Normal grants fall in the $1000-$2500 range and are not renewable.

21st Century Community Learning Centers Program
http://www.ed.gov/21stcclc/
The No Child Left Behind Act converted the 21st Century Community Learning Centers program, an after school initiative, from a federally administered discretionary grants program to a state-administered program.

Afterschool.Gov Finding Federal Dollars
http://www.afterschool.gov/feddollar1.html
This database gives you one stop for information about more than 100 sources of federal funding for after-school and youth development programming.

Allstate Foundation
http://www.allstate.com/foundation/funding.html
Education grants are in the area of personal safety and security and include after-school programs with initiatives that safeguard against gangs and delinquency, fire safety, child safety advocacy, and anti-drinking and driving programs. Public schools and private/charter schools, but not private secondary schools, have received grants.

American Association of University Women (AAUW)
Community Action Grants
http://www.aauw.org/fga/fellowships_grants/community_action.cfm
Offers Community Action Grants, which provide seed money to individual women, AAUW branches, AAUW state organizations, and local community-based nonprofit organizations for innovative programs.

American Education Research Association (AERA) Grants Program
http://www.aera.net/grantsprogram/
The AERA Grants Program invites proposals for quantitative education policy research using large-scale, nationally-representative data sets such as those sponsored by NCES and NSF. Minority researchers are strongly encouraged to apply.

American Express Economic Independence Fund
http://www.nefe.org/amexeconfundrfp/aeeif2004rfp.html
Any U.S. nonprofit organization designated as a 501(c)(3) by the IRS whose clients are representative of underserved audiences targeted by The Fund and who would benefit from financial literacy education is eligible to apply.

Ameritech Technology Academy
http://www.ameritechacademy.org/
More than 2000 Michigan teachers are to receive intensive computer training during the next two years thanks to a $2 million grant from Ameritech. Teams of teachers from about 400 schools will attend the Ameritech Technology Academy, then return to their institutions to pass along their knowledge.

Amica Insurance Grants for High Alcohol-Free Post-Prom and Post-Graduation Parties
http://www.amica.com/
Through its Save the Night program, Amica Mutual Insurance Company is offering grants to high schools across the United States for planning safe, alcohol-free post-prom and post-graduation parties. For complete guidelines and to submit an

online application, see the company's Web site. Contact: Amica's Save the Night Program, Patricia O'Hara, Tel: (800) 622-6422 ext. 2100.

Anderson Reflections Arts Enhancement Grant Program (Mary Lou)
http://www.pta.org//parentinvolvement/familyfun/mla.asp
A limited number of matching grants of up to $1,000 are awarded each year to local PTAs for student-centered programs focused on arts education.

Apple iLife Educator Awards
http://www.apple.com/education/ilifeawards/
Teachers who creatively use iLife applications to enhance lessons, exceed instructional standards, and meet the needs of today's students are encouraged to submit their lesson plans for consideration.

AT&T Foundation Education Grants
http://www.att.com/foundation/
The foundation's scope is national, emphasizing support of higher education and institutions and national organizations serving the academic community, and K-12 education. Areas of funding under this category include programs/projects that use technology to enhance teaching and learning, encourage family involvement in schools, provide professional development opportunities for educators, prepare future teachers for the learning environment, and implement plans for lifelong learning and community collaboration.

Autodesk Inc./ITEA Elementary Grants
http://www.iteawww.org/I2a.html
Autodesk Inc. and the The International Technology Education Association have partnered to promote the new basic in our elementary schools—technology education. All elementary schools (K-6) are invited to become involved in the technology education movement with technology activities and applying to this year's grants program.

Beaumont Foundation of America Technology Grants
http://www.bmtfoundation.com
For technology development in underserved schools. Between 100-350 grants ranging from $60,000 to $20,000. K-12 public schools are eligible if 50 percent of its students qualify for the National School Lunch Program. For more information, call (800) 505-2667.

BellSouth Foundation Opportunity Grants
http://www.bellsouthfoundation.org/
The fundamental mission of the foundation is to stimulate far-reaching and lasting improvements in the results achieved by public K-12 education in southeastern United States.

Beloit, Wisconsin Office of Grants and Home Programs
http://www.sdb.k12.wi.us/grants/
Includes grant postings of interest to elementary and secondary educators.

Blockbuster Community Relations
http://www.blockbuster.com/bb/about/bbcommunityrelations/0,7701,NT-ABT,00.html
Blockbuster sponsors several programs that use movies both to teach and reward students in schools across the U.S. More than 11,000 elementary schools are also taking part in our BLOCKBUSTER Class Act Award program, which allows elementary school teachers to reward their students' efforts with free movie rentals from BLOCKBUSTER.

Box Tops for Education
http://www.boxtops4education.com/
Box Tops for Education has donated over $90 million to our nation's schools since 1996, helping them earn the cash they need through easy, everyday activities. Join the Box Tops Booster Club to earn more for your school…and do something good for your family, too. Courtesy of General Mills.

Bush Foundation for Family Literacy (Barbara)
http://www.barbarabushfoundation.com/nga.html
The goal of the national grant program is to develop and expand family literacy efforts nationwide, and to support the development of literacy programs that build families of readers. A total of $500,000 is awarded each year; no grant exceeds $50,000.

Campbell's Labels for Education
http://www.labelsforeducation.com/index.asp
"Labels for Education™" is an easy, fun way to help schools in your neighborhood get free educational merchandise, including computers, sports equipment and musical instruments. sponsored by Campbell's Soups.

Carnegie Corporation of New York Eduction Program
http://www.carnegie.org/sub/program/education.html
Funding priorities include early childhood education, urban school reform, and higher education.

Casey Foundation (Annie E.)
http://www.aecf.org

Center for Education Reform
Grant Alert
http://www.edreform.com/info/grant.htm
Information on grants available for teachers, school programs and education reform initiatives.

Character Education Partnership
National Schools of Character Award Grants
http://character.org/eventsawards/nsoc
Provides awards of $2,000 to K-12 public schools who have been teaching character education initiatives that yield positive results in student behavior and academic performance. Must emphasize ethical values.

Charter School Dissemination Grants
http://www.charterschooldissemination.org/pages/index.cfm
Dissemination grants are provided for under the Charter Schools Program (CSP). The CSP was originally authorized in 1994 under Title X, Part C of the Elementary and Secondary Education Act of 1965. State Education Agencies may use CSP funds to award subgrants to charter schools in the State. Dissemination grants are awarded to charter schools to support activities that help open new public schools or share the lessons learned by charter schools with other public schools.

CocaCola Foundation
http://www2.coca-cola.com/citizenship/foundation.html
The Foundation supports programs in higher education, classroom teaching and learning, and international education. Our programs support scholarships for aspiring students; encourage and motivate young people to stay in school; and foster cultural understanding.

Computers for Learning (GSA)
http://www.computers.fed.gov/Public/home.asp

The CFL program places computers in our classrooms and prepares our children to contribute and compete in the 21st century. The program transfers excess Federal computer equipment to schools and educational nonprofit organizations, giving special consideration to those with the greatest need.

Dirksen Congressional Center
Robert H. Michel Civic Education Grants
http://www.dirksencenter.org/grantmichelciviced.htm
The Dirksen Congressional Center invites applications for grants totaling $35,000 in 2004 to help teachers, curriculum developers, and others improve the quality of civics instruction, with priority on the role of Congress in our federal government.

The Dollywood Foundation
http://www.dollywoodfoundation.com
The Dollywood Foundation is a 501(c)(3) nonprofit organization founded in 1988 by Dolly Parton and the Dollywood Company. Committed to helping children Dream More, Learn More, Care More and Be More, the Dollywood Foundation develops and administers educational programs for children locally in Dolly's native Sevier County, Tennessee as well as nationwide.

Education Grants/Programs Available from the U.S. Government
Posted on the Catalog of Federal Domestic Assistance
http://www.cfda.gov/public/grantsubtopic.asp?catcode=G
Subcategories include: Dental Education and Training, Educational Equipment and Resources, Educational Facilities, Elementary and Secondary, General Research and Evaluation, Handicapped Education, Health Education and Training, Higher Education—General, Indian Education, Libraries and Technical Information Services, Medical Education and Training, Nuclear Education and Training, Nursing Education, Resource Development and Support—Elementary, Secondary Education, Resource Development and Support—General and Special Interest Organizations, Resource Development and Support—Higher Education, Resource Development and Support—Land and Equipment, Resource Development and Support—School Aid, Resource Development and Support—Sciences, Resource Development and Support—Student Financial Aid, Resource Development and Support—Vocational Education and Handicapped Education, Teacher Training, and Vocational Development.

Education Grants/Programs from the U.S. Government
Posted on Grants.gov
http://www.grants.gov/FindGrantOpportunities
Some of the most current grant opportunities posted by the federal government.

Education Place Grants and Funding Opportunities
http://www.eduplace.com/grants/
Courtesy of Houghton Mifflin, this web page is divided into three sections: Grants for Houghton Mifflin products, available grants and links, and help with grant writing including sample grant proposals that won funding.

EDUCYBER Educator's Grants Information Page
http://www.educyber.com/educator/grants.php

ESCHOOLNEWS Online Funding Center
http://www.eSchoolNews.org/resources/funding/
Provides tips on funding and technology opportunities. Also markets a funding directory.

EXWORTHY Educational Links
Grants, Funding, and Donations
http://www.exworthy.com/
Find educational technology grants, e-rate updates and forms, grant applications, grant writing guides, and hardware purchasing/donation information at these links.

Federal Funding Opportunities for Education Grants/Programs Posted on Grants.gov
http://www.grants.gov/FindGrantOpportunities
Lists some of the most recent grant programs available.

FedGrants Federal Funding Opportunities
http://www.fedgrants.gov/Applicants/index.html
Funding opportunities from the U.S. Department of Education (ED) are sorted by a variety of ways including date posted and elibility status.

Foundations and Organizations that Support Education Innovation
http://www.ed.gov/about/offices/list/oii/resources/foundations.html

Fund for Teachers
Professional Development Grants,br> http://www.fundforteachers.org/
The Fund for Teachers provides grants of up to $5,000 to classroom teachers with a minimum of three years experience, so that they may participate in training and enriching activities that will improve and enhance their skills as teachers.

Funding for Afterschool
http://www.afterschool.org/funding.cfm

FundingFactory Recycling Program
http://www.etcep.com/
FundingFactory has helped thousands of educational and non-profit organizations nationwide reach their fundraising goals in an effective and innovative way…recycling. Your organization can earn FREE technology, sports & recreation equipment, playground systems or even CASH by simply collecting and recycling items most people just throw away. Recycle empty inkjet & laser cartridges and even old cell phones and start redeeming your rewards immediately.

Fundsnet Services Online Education Corporate Funders
http://www.fundsnetservices.com/educ01.htm

Fundsnet Services Online Education Grantmaking Foundations
http://www.fundsnetservices.com/educatio.htm

Gates Foundation (Bill and Melinda)
http://www.gatesfoundation.org/
Bill and Melinda Gates hope to make an enduring contribution toward increasing access to innovations in education, technology, and global health. More than seventeen billion dollars in endowments have been set aside for these causes.

Gear Up Program
Gaining Early Awareness and Readiness for Undergraduate Programs
http://www.ed.gov/programs/gearup/index.html
The GEAR UP program is a discretionary grant program designed to increase the number of low-income students who are prepared to enter and succeed in postsecondary education.

General Mills Box Tops for Education
http://www.boxtops4education.com/

A nationwide fundraising program that helps K-8 schools earn extra cash for items that are not covered by shrinking school budgets. With Box Tops for Education, your school can earn up to $10,000 in cash for new playground equipment. Library books. Technology. Art supplies. Whatever your school needs most!

Globe Science and Education Program
http://www.globe.gov/fsl/html/templ.cgi?nsfao&lang=en&nav=1
GLOBE is a hands-on, school-based science and education program. In the U.S., GLOBE is a Federal interagency program sponsored by NOAA, NASA, NSF, and EPA, in partnership with over 140 colleges and universities, state and local school systems and non-government organizations.

Good Neighbor Service-Learning Award
http://www.ysa.org/pdffiles/2003_GN.pdf
The State Farm Good Neighbor Service-Learning Award enables youth and educators to bring positive benefits of service-learning to more young people.

Grants and Other Funding Opportunities
http://learn.arc.nasa.gov/grants/index.html
A compilation of resources for K-12 grade teachers provided by the NASA Learning Technologies Project.

Grants.gov : Current Federal Funding Opportunities for Education
http://www.grants.gov/FindGrantOpportunities

Help Us Help Foundation
http://www.helpushelp.org
With financial support provided by database software giant Oracle Corporation, the nonprofit Help Us Help Foundation assists K-12 public schools and youth organizations in economically challenged communities to obtain information technology tools. Grants of computer equipment and software are available to schools and youth organizations in the U.S. that provide educational programs in low-income communities.

Hewlett-Packard Company K-8 Science Support
http://h21030.www2.hp.com/us/programs/science_leadership.html
Through the HP Science Leadership strategic grant initiative, HP supports attendance of U.S. K-8 school district teams from low-income, ethnically diverse communities at National Science Resources Center (NSRC) Institutes.

Hot Grant Bytes
http://www.gisd.k12.mi.us/grants/hotbytes.htm
Presents potential financial resources for educators, updated daily by Genesee
Intermediate School District's Grants & Development Department.

IBM Corporate Grants
http://www.ibm.com/ibm/ibmgives/grant/education/
Description: The primary grant-making focus is public education on a national
basis with emphasis on areas of company operations including Armond, NY. Also
gives products and employee matching gifts.

IndiVisual Learning LLC/Hewlett Packard Read for Life Scholarships
http://www.indivisuallearning.com/scholarship.html?refer=www.fundsnetservices.com
IndiVisual Learning LLC, a provider of engaging academic intervention programs, in co-sponsorship with Hewlett-Packard Co., will award $25,000 'Read
for Life' Scholarships to two deserving public, private, charter, or parochial
schools throughout the country.

Intel Public Affairs Contribution and Grant Information
http://www.intel.com/community/grant.htm
Our primary giving focus is education; we have strong interest in supporting K-
12/higher education and community programs that deliver the kind of educational opportunities that all students will need to prepare themselves to succeed
in the 21st century. Intel vigorously supports education through grants for programs that advance science, math and technology education, particularly for
women and underserved populations.

INTEL's Global Commitment to Education
http://www.intel.com/education/sections/corporate1/index.htm
http://www.intel.com/education/sections/corporate3/index.htm

International Reading Association
Regie Routman Teacher Recognition Award
http://www.ira.org/awards/regierou.html
Deadline: Completed entries must be received by November 1.
The Regie Routman Teacher Recognition Award honors an outstanding regular
classroom elementary teacher of reading and language arts in grades K-6 (ages 5-
12) dedicated to improving teaching and learning through reflective writing
about his or her teaching and learning process. The US$1,000 award is supported
by a grant from Regie Routman. All applicants must be Association members.

JCPenney Corporate Giving Program
http://www.jcpenneyinc.com/company/commrel/index.htm
J.C. Penney grants focus on improvement of K through 12th grade education through curriculum-based after school care, with a priority on JCPenney Afterschool. Grants usually range from $100 to $5000.

Joyce Foundation
http://www.joycefdn.org/

Kellogg Foundation Learning Initiatives for Young Children and Adolescents
http://www.wkkf.org
Two initiatives—SPARK: Supporting Partnerships to Assure Ready Kids and New Options for Youth Through Engaged Institutions—will be launched immediately by the foundation, which plans to contribute $10 million toward their development over the next decade.

Knight Foundation
http://www.knightfdn.org/
This foundation emphacizes four major program areas: Community Initiatives, Journalism, Education, and Arts and Culture.

Kohl's Fundraising Card Program
http://www.kohlscorporation.com/CommunityRelations/Community04.htm
The Kohl's Cares for Kids® Fundraising Card Program benefits school and non-profit youth organizations through the use of special gift cards.

Kurzwell Educational Systems
Teacher Resources—Funding Information Sources for Assistive Technology
http://kurzweiledu.com/proof_resources_funding.asp

Laubach Literacy—National Book Scholarship Fund
http://www.laubach.org/NBSF/indexnbs.html
The purpose of the National Book Scholarship Fund (NBSF), is to distribute direct in-kind assistance to local literacy providers throughout the United States.

Lesko's Job Help (Matthew)
http://www.lesko.com/help/JobHelp.htm
Money, information and services find a new career or get satisfaction in a current one.

Liberty Mutual Corporate Giving Program
http://www.libertymutual.com/omapps/ContentServer?pagename=CorporateInternet/
Page/StandardTeal&cid=1003349317246&dir=/CorporateInternet/CorpHomePage/
CorpAboutLibertyMutual/CorpCommunityAction
The Liberty Mutual Group Corporate Philanthropy Program supports nonprofit
organizations that help people live safer, more secure lives in communities
throughout the U.S. where the company has employees and customers. The company also provides support in the areas of education, with priority on programs
for disadvantaged youth, and health and safety.

Lisa Libraries
http://www.lisalibraries.org/frames.html
The Lisa Libraries donates new children's books and small libraries to organizations that work with kids in poor and underserved areas.

Lowe's Community Giving
http://www.lowes.com/lkn?action=pg&p=AboutLowes/Community#charitable
Lowe's Charitable and Educational Foundation awards more than $1.5 million
annually to individuals and organizations across the United States. The
Foundation considers requests only from 501(c)(3) organizations.

Lumina Foundation for Education
http://www.luminafoundation.org/
A private, independent foundation, strives to help people achieve their potential
by expanding access and success in education beyond high school.
Matthew Lesko, see Lesko

MEDTRONIC Foundation Star Grants
http://www.medtronic.com/foundation/star.html
STAR aims to increase science learning by all students and to provide them with the
opportunity to consider careers in science, health, engineering and technical fields.

MEEMIC Foundation for the Future of Education Minigrant Program
http://www.meemic.com/comfndoverCKR.htm
Application form
The MEEMIC Foundation for the Future of Education, a non-profit organization created in 1992 by the MEEMIC Insurance Company offers financial assistance to schools and educators in the form of mini-grants. For more information,
write the MEEMIC Foundation Mini Grant Program, 691 N. Squirrel Rd. Suite

100, Auburn Hills, Michigan 48326; Email: foundation@meemic.com; Phone: (248) 375-7535; Fax: (248) 375-7549

Michel Civic Education Grants for Teachers of Grades 6-12 (Robert H.)
http://www.dirksencenter.org/grantmichelciviced.htm
The Dirksen Congressional Center provides grants to develop practical classroom strategies to improve the quality of teaching and learning about civics with a particular emphasis on the role of Congress in the federal government. Grants are intended to help teachers, curriculum developers, and others improve the quality of civics instruction. Both public school and private/charter schools are elibible. $35,000 available. For more information contact us at fmackaman@pdkin.net

Microsoft Innovative Teachers Education Grant
http://www.microsoft.com/Education/?ID=InTeachersGrant
Nearly $50 million in software licenses and online community-building tools will be awarded to schools, colleges, and departments of education that partner with local school districts. The goal: Provide technology-related professional development opportunities to faculty members, prospective teachers, and practicing teachers.

National Association for the Exchange of Industrial Resources
http://www.naeir.org/
Collects donations of overstocked and discontinued merchandise from businesses and redistributes them to schools and non-profit groups.

National Charter School Clearinghouse
Funding Links
http://www.ncsc.info/mod.php?mod=userpage&menu=8&page_id=1
Provides links to a variety of resources of potential value to grant seekers. Resources are divided into the following sections: Cause Related Marketing, Corporate/Other Opportunities, Federal, Foundation, Grant Tips, Grant Writing Assistance, Grantwriter Database, State, and Successful Proposals.

National Council for the Social Studies
CivConnections Grants
http://www.socialstudies.org/civiconnections
Grants for public school teacher teams and students grades 3-12 to link historical inquiry with community service-learning projects. Thirty-three teams of teachers are expected to be funded with an average grant of $7500.

National Education Association
Youth Leaders for Literacy
http://www.nea.org/readacross/volunteer/youthleaders.html
Grants for student-led initiatives at public and private/charter schools for reading-related activities that benefit others. Students must be between the ages of 5 and 21. Average grant amount: $500.00

National School Fitness Foundation
http://www.fitnessfoundation.org/
Schools that have an extra 1,800 square feet and interested staff members could qualify for free athletic equipment, including weight machines and computers that measure body fat and heart rates. The offer, valued at $200,000 to $250,000 per school, comes from the National School Fitness Foundation, a Utah-based nonprofit organization that seeks to increase physical activity among school children.

National Institute for Literacy Grants and Funding Sources
http://www.nifl.gov/

National School Safety and Security Services
Tips for Funding School Safety and Security Services
http://www.schoolsecurity.org/resources/funding.html

National Teaching and Learning Forum
Teaching and Learning Grant Opportunities
http://www.ntlf.com/html/grants/titles.htm
The Oryx Press, co-publisher of The National Teaching and Learning Forum, has one of the most comprehensive databases of grants information available anywhere. From that database, we have culled this selection of 37 grants which should be of interest to faculty and instructional development specialists and to faculty with an interest in teaching and curriculum development.

National Weather Association
Sol Hirsch Education Fund Grants
http://www.nwas.org/solhirsch.html
$500 grants are available annually for teachers in grades K-12 to improve the education of their students in Meteorology.

NEC's Corporate Citizenship
http://www.nec.co.jp/community/en/

Makes cash grants to nonprofit organizations and programs with national reach and impact in one or both of the following arenas: science and technology education, principally at the secondary level, and/or the application of technology to assist people with disabilities.

NetDay Compass Guide to Educational Funding
http://www.netdaycompass.org/categories.cfm?instance_id=1718&category_id=3
Provides a directory of foundations and other organizations that provide funding to support education.

Newman's Own Charitable Foundation
http://www.newmansown.com/5_good.html
Offers grants to nonprofits, schools, hospitals, and other 501(c)(3) public benefit organizations. Eligible grant categories include: the arts, children and youth, health, education, the elderly, environment, the handicapped, literacy, substance abuse education, programs for the needy including housing and food, but no funding for individuals or scholarships.

News for Educators Online Now (NEON)
http://www.itrc.ucf.edu/neon/archives/archives.html
Includes information about grant opporunities.

North American Moose Foundation
Grants for Middle Schools
http://www.moosefoundation.org/home.htm
The North American Moose Foundation is pleased to announce the availability of 8 (eight) individual $250 grants, for Middle Schools, grades 6, 7, or 8, in the U.S. and Canada.

Oracle Help Us Help Foundation
http://www.helpushelp.org/
A nonprofit organization that assists K-12 public schools and youth organizations in economically challenged communities through grants of computer equipment and software. Our funding comes from Oracle Corporation, and we are supported by charitable donations from individuals and other corporations as well.

Otto Seeds for Education Grant Program (Lorri)
http://www.for-wild.org/seedmony.htm

Provides small monetary grants to schools, nature centers, or other non-profit educational organizations for the purpose of establishing outdoor learning centers. Encourages use of wild flowers.

Palm Beach County School District
Office of Research & Development
Grant Opportunities Page
http://www.palmbeach.k12.fl.us/ord/opportunities.htm

Palm Education Pioneer Program
http://palmgrants.sri.com/grants.html
The goal of the Palm Education Pioneers program is to enable exploration and evaluation of innovative uses of Palm handheld computers for K-12 learning, through classroom grants to teachers.

PEP National Directory of Computer Recycling Programs
http://web.archive.org/web/20030713042128/
http://microweb.com/pepsite/Recycle/recycle_index.html
A state, national and international directory of agencies that facilitate donations of used computer hardware for schools and community groups sponsored by Resources for Parents, Educators, and Publishers (PEP).

PEW Grant Program in Course Redesign
http://www.center.rpi.edu/infoappl.html

Playground Equipment Fundraising Ideas
http://www.jenningsmi.com/fundraising.htm
Features the playground dance, cocktail and appetizer party, plant and garden sale, pizza week, selling t-shirts, playground campaign, general raffle, pasta dinner, school fair or carnival, and benefit concert. Sponsored by Jennings of Michigan Playground Equipment.

Potential Resources for Playground Safety Funding
http://www.uni.edu/playground/resources/funding.html
This web site, sponsored by the University of Northern Iowa National Program for Playground Safety, identifies funders who may assist in providing safer playground equipment for schools and other public facilities.

Preparing Tomorrow's Teachers to Use Technology Grants
http://www.ed.gov/teachtech/

PT3 grants support innovative program improvements to prepare technology-proficient educators for 21st century schools.

Resource Guide to Federal Funding for Technology in Education
http://www.ed.gov/Technology/tec-guid.html
A detailed explanation of the grants available for technology as well as a list of additional funding sources for hardware and software.

Rockefeller Brother Fund Education Program
http://www.rbf.org
The goals of the Rockefeller Brothers Fund are to promote universal, quality education and care for pre-kindergarten children throughout the U.S. and to increase the number of talented and committed minority teachers in the United States public education system. There is no deadline for this Rockefeller Brothers Fund program. For more information contact: Benjamin R. Shute, Jr., 212-812-4200, email: rock@rbf.org.

Rural Assistance Center
Education and Training Funding
http://www.raconline.org/info_guides/education/index.php#funding

Rural Assistance Center
School Funding
http://www.raconline.org/info_guides/schools/index.php

Rural School and Community Trust
http://www.ruralchallenge.org/
The Rural Challenge provides grants to rural schools striving for educational reform.

SAMI, see Science and Math Initiatives.

San Mateo County (California) Office of Education
Grant Annoucements
http://www.smcoe.k12.ca.us/ssfusd/do/DOResources/Grants.html
Regularly reports grant opportunities for teachers and schools.

Scholastic Programs, Awards, and Grants
http://www.scholastic.com/aboutscholastic/community/index.htm

Each year, Scholastic reinforces its commitment to literacy and learning with numerous awards programs designed to inspire and reward excellence, among students and educators.

School Funding Services Grant of the Week

http://www.schoolfundingservices.org/newsViewer.asp?docId=2546
Each week School Funding Services, a division of New American Schools, features a new grant on their website.

Smarter Kids Foundation

http://www.smarterkids.org/
The SMARTer Kids Foundation is a private organization that provides opportunities for students and teachers to learn new skills and grow in self-confidence by placing technology, grants and programs at their service. The Foundation helps equip classrooms with technology products and generates practical research on the impact and effectiveness of technology in the classroom.

Staples Foundation for Learning

http://www.staplesfoundation.org/foundapplication.html
The mission of Staples Foundation for Learning is to provide funding to programs that support or provide job skills and/or education for all people, with a special emphasis on disadvantaged youth.

Starbucks Foundation

http://www.starbucks.com/aboutus/grantinfo.asp
Description: Education grants to award literacy grants to organizations promoting pre-reading and pre-school experiences with language and literature that will enable a child to succeed in school on a national basis in areas where the company has retail stores. Mini-grants of up to $1,000 for literacy projects and opportunity grants up to $10,000. For more information, call (206) 447-1575, ext. 87022.

State Farm Foundation

http://www.statefarm.com/foundati/cogrants.htm
The State Farm Companies Foundation makes charitable contributions to nonprofit, tax-exempt organizations under Section 501(c)(3) of the U.S. Internal Revenue Code, Canadian charitable organizations, and educational institutions.

StudyWwb Education Foundation and Grants

http://www.studyweb.com/

Click on Education on the left and then "Foundations and Grants" for an extensive list of resources for school teachers and administrators.

Target Arts in Education Grants
http://target.com/target_group/community_giving/arts_in_education_grants.jhtml

Target School Fundraising Program
http://target.com/target_group/schools/search_school.jhtml
Have one per cent of your Target Credit Card charges go to a designated school.

A Teacher's Guide to Fellowships and Awards
http://www.doe.mass.edu/tgfa/default.html
Funding opportunities are sorted out into the following categories: Arts; Business, Industry and Economics; Educational Improvement; Educational Leadership; English/Language Arts; Excellence in Teaching; History/Social Studies; Humanities; International Studies; Library Science and Media; Mathematics and Science; Research; Technology; and World Languages.

Teacher Laptop Foundation
http://www.teacherlaptop.org/
A national 501(c)(3) nonprofit charitable organization collecting donations to provide laptops to teachers.

Teacher Resource Guide on Science Resource Grants
http://www.venturesfoundation.org/pubs/other/Teacher%20Resource%20Guide%20SCIENCE.pdf
A guide for classroom teachers containing most popular requests & common rejections to give teachers ideas for requests and make the process easier. Compiled by Philanthropic Ventures Foundation for California elementary and secondary schools.

TeachersNetwork.Org
Grants for Teachers, Educators, and Students
http://teachersnetwork.org/grants/default.htm
TeacherNetwork.org staff and teacher web mentors offer information on grants and other resources. Categories include: humanities, math, science, social studies, scholarships, technology, etc.

Teaching Tolerance Grant Program
http://www.tolerance.org/teach/expand/gra/guide.jsp

The Teaching Tolerance project of the Southern Poverty Law Center offers grants of up to $2,000 to K-12 classroom teachers for implementing tolerance and youth activism projects in their schools and communities.

TechLearning.com Grants and Contests
http://www.techlearning.com/grants.html
Provides a directory of awards, grants, and funding opportunities available for schools and teachers. Some of the grants may be useful for obtaining technology.

Time Warner Foundation
http://www.timewarner.com/public_service/time_warner_foundation/foundation.adp
The Foundation makes grants to: * National and community-based after-school organizations which engage creative and media arts and prepare underserved teens for college; * Organizations that work to raise awareness of the need for quality after-school programs. * Efforts to foster leadership opportunities for public school students in selected cities.

Top 50 U.S. Foundations Awarding Grants in Education, 1999
http://fdncenter.org/fc_stats/subject01_99.html
Also provides breakouts for Elementary and Secondary Education, Higher Education, and Graduate and Professional Education. Courtesy of the Foundation Center.

Top 50 U.S. Foundations Awarding Grants in Education, 2001
http://fdncenter.org/fc_stats/pdf/04_fund_sub/2001/50_found_sub/f_sub_b20_01.pdf

Toshiba America Foundation
Science and Math Education Grants
http://www.toshiba.com/taf/
The mission of the Toshiba America Foundation is to contribute to the quality of science and mathematics education in U.S. communities by investing in projects designed by classroom teachers to improve science and mathematics education for students in grades K-12. The Foundation offers two grants programs, one focused on K-6 science and math education and one focused on 7-12 science and math education.

Toyota's Investment In Mathematics Excellence (TIME)
http://www.nctm.org/about/toyota/index.asp

A grant awarding teachers up to $10,000 for innovative projects that enhance mathematics education within a school.

U.S. Department of Education
Financial Aid Page
http://www.ed.gov/topics/topics.jsp?&top=Financial+Aid

U.S. Department of Education
Grants and Contracts Page
http://www.ed.gov/fund/landing.jhtml

U.S. Department of Education
Office of Educational Technology
http://www.ed.gov/Technology/
Through projects initiated under the Improving America's Schools Act and through long-term programs, the Department of Education promotes the use of technology in schools, libraries, and communities to achieve its mission of ensuring equal access to education and promoting educational excellence throughout the nation.

U.S. Department of Education
Office of Innovation and Improvement
Funding Opportunities
http://www.ed.gov/about/offices/list/oii/funding.html
The Office of Innovation and Improvement (OII) administers about 25 discretionary grant programs that foster education innovation at the state and local levels.

U.S. Department of Education
Office of Migrant Education
http://www.ed.gov/about/offices/list/oese/ome/index.html
Describes funding opportunities available for state governments from this Department of Education Office of Elementary and Secondary Education subagency.

U.S. Department of Education
Office of Postsecondary Schools (OSE)
http://www.ed.gov/about/offices/list/ope/programs.html
The Office of Postsecondary Education (OPE) administers over 40 programs that address critical national needs and support our mission of increasing access to quality postsecondary education.

Veritas Grants and Donations Programs
http://www.veritas.com/aboutus/foundation/Foundation.jhtml
The VERITAS Foundation provides grants to organizations that meet the
Foundation's policies and grant guidelines, are recommended by the Foundation
Council, and are approved by the Foundation Board of Directors.

Verizon's Extra Credit for School Program
http://www.verizonld.com/ECFS/
Verizon will set aside 5% of your monthly long distance usage to benefit K-12
education in your area. Each quarter, your school, district, or educational foundation will receive a royalty check. Contributions are automatically made in your
name, and you invest no money.

Wallace Foundation
http://www.wallacefoundation.org/WF/GrantsPrograms/
The Wallace Foundation funds educational projects in two different areas: *To
develop effective educational leadership, especially among principals and superin-
tendents, to improve student learning. *To improve the quality of out-of-school
learning opportunities for children and families and to promote learning as a core
community value.

WalMart Foundation
http://www.walmartfoundation.org/
Through its community involvement program, WalMart provides funding to a
number of nonprofits working in the areas of children, community, education,
and environment. WalMart also provides scholarships to associates.

Walton Family Foundation Inc.
Grants for Charter Schools and Charter School Developers
http://www.wffhome.com/program_focus.htm
The Foundation makes charter school grants available in the following states: AR,
AZ, CA, CO, D.C., FL, IL, MA, MI, MN, MO, NY, OH, OR, and WI,
although we consider making Planning Grants to applicants within most all charter states with active charter laws.

Washington Mutual Corporate Giving
http://www.wamu.com/about/community/programs/wamueducation/wamueducation.htm
Washington Mutual, a banking and financial services company, seeks to make the
communities it serves stronger through grants supporting K-12 public education,
financial education and affordable housing.

WEBHANDS.ORG
http://www.webhands.org
A directory of organizations providing food, clothing, homeless shelter, literacy assistance, and help bridging the digital divide. Courtesy of General Motors.

World Wide Christian Schools
http://www.gospelcom.net/wcs/
This public charity in Grand Rapids, MI provides funding to churches and other stable, accountable nonprofits to build schools in Third World nations. Support is provided only for Christian education-related projects and programs. The organization is primarily focused on economically disadvantaged children who have limited opportunity for education.

GRANTS FOR NONPROFITS

GOVERNMENT FUNDING

Catalog of Federal Domestic Assistance
http://www.cfda.gov/
This web site gives you access to a database of all Federal programs available to State and local governments (including the District of Columbia); federally-recognized Indian tribal governments; Territories (and possessions) of the United States; domestic public, quasi-public, and private profit and nonprofit organizations and institutions; specialized groups; and individuals. You can search this database to find assistance programs meeting your requirements and for which you are eligible. You can then contact the office that administers the program and find out how to apply.

Faith-Based & Community Initiatives
http://www.hhs.gov/fbci/
The President's Faith-Based and Community Initiative does not fund religion—but it does allow some of America's most effective social service providers to compete for Federal funding to serve the needy while retaining their religious identity. Through soup kitchens, homeless shelters, drug treatment centers, job training programs, and other efforts, these charities are making a real difference in the lives of our most vulnerable citizens.

Federal Funding Tools and Information Sources
http://www.lib.msu.edu/harris23/grants/federal.htm
Provides web links to federal databases, newsletters, and websites.

FirstGov Business and Nonprofit Gateway
http://www.firstgov.gov/Business/Nonprofit.shtml
Access portal for grant information for business and nonprofits.

FirstGov State and Local Gateway to Grants and Government Information
http://www.firstgov.gov/Government/State_Local.shtml
Access portal for grant information for state and local governments.

FirstGov Surplus Property Links
http://www.firstgov.gov/shopping/forgovernment/forgovernment.shtml

GovLoans.gov
http://govloans.gov/govloans/
"Five federal agencies—U.S. Department of Agriculture, U.S. Department of Education, U.S. Department of Housing and Urban Development, U.S. Small Business Administration, and the U.S. Department of Veterans Affairs—have come together to create this single point of access for federal loan information on the Web." Browse or search for loans for farming, businesses, students, disaster relief, and more. Includes a glossary of loan terms and links to additional resources.

Grants.gov Grant Portal
http://grants.gov/
Grants.gov provides organizations with the ability to search for Federal government-wide grant opportunities. If you are an individual looking for information on government benefits, refer to GovBenefits.gov, the official government benefits website, a free, confidential tool that helps individuals find government benefits they may be eligible to receive.

Grants Information for Constituents
http://www.house.gov/israel/grants/crs-rs20514-092203.pdf
This report describes key sources of information on government and private grants for state and community projects.

USDA Nonprofit Gateway
http://www.usda.gov/nonprofi.htm
Lists sources of funding for rural areas.

GRANTS FOR NONPROFITS

BUSINESS AND ECONOMIC DEVELOPMENT

4 Proven Ways to Use Credit to Jump-start Your Startup!
http://www.office.com/templates/page1.asp?docid=88
So you're ready to take the plunge and go out on you own but you're low on funds. Not to worry. Many successful businesses have started under similar circumstances—jump started by credit! Here are four proven ways to jump-start your business.

5 Ways to Get Angel Money
http://www.office.com/templates/page1.asp?docid=83
Thinking of Angel Funding? Check out these 5 tips!

About.com's Guide to Funding for Inventors
http://inventors.about.com/msub4.htm?once=true&

America's Business Funding Directory
http://www.businessfinance.com
Venture capital is harder to find these days than a Pac-Man machine. This site is designed to put visitors in touch with potential investors and financing sources. There's an easy-to-use search engine, a selection of financing workbooks, a resource library and links to business software resources and small business development centers.

Bank of America Corporation
http://www.bankofamerica.com/community/
Bank of America is recognized as a national leader in the community development industry. This leadership role is based on results that have helped bring positive change to communities through the development of affordable housing, the

financing of small businesses and the identification of new ways in which Bank of America can use creativity, partnerships and expertise to help communities thrive.

Borrowing Money for Your Business
http://web.archive.org/web/20011115231324/
http://www.tsbj.com/editorial/03040702.htm

Business and Commerce Grants from the U.S. Government
Posted on Catalog of Federal Domestic Assistance (CFDA)
http://www.cfda.gov/public/grantsubtopic.asp?catcode=B
Subcategories include: Maritime, Statistics, Special Services, Minority Business Enterprises, Small Business, Economic Development, Economic Injury and Natural Disaster, Commercial Fisheries, and International.

Business and Commerce Grants from the U.S. Government
Posted on Grants.gov
http://www.grants.gov/FindGrantOpportunities
Some of the most current grant opportunities posted by the federal government.

Business Owner's Idea Cafe Grant Center
http://www.businessownersideacafe.com/business_grants/index.html
Provides information on obtaining grants from various funders, including the federal government. Idea Central also provides a few small grants.

BusinessFinance.com
http://www.businessfinance.com/
A commerical web site that provides categorized funding criteria for over 4,000 sources of business capital.

Catalog of Federal Domestic Assistance
Minority Business Enterprises Grant Programs
http://www.cfda.gov/public/browse_sub.asp?subcode=BS&st=1

Catalog of Federal Domestic Assistance
Small Business Development Grant Programs
http://www.cfda.gov/public/browse_sub.asp?subcode=BK&st=1

Count Me in For Women's Economic Independence
http://www.count-me-in.org/

An internet-based organization that raises money to make small-business loans to women.

Entreworld.org's Business Financing
http://entreworld.org/Channel/SYB.cfm?topic=finc
The Kaufmann Foundation sponsors this web page which is divided into the following business finance sections: conventional sources, loans, investments, angel, venture capital, and alternative sources.

Fedbizzopps.gov
http://www.eps.gov/
Review federal business opportunities posted over the last 30 days.

Federal Funding Opportunities for Business and Commerce Posted on Grants.gov
http://www.grants.gov/FindGrantOpportunities
Lists the most recently posted grants.

Financing Options for Start-Up Manufacturers
http://www.office.com/templates/page1.asp?docid=22

Financing Your Business
http://www.sba.gov/financing/
Describes the various loan programs of the U.S. Small Business Administration.

GovLoans.gov
http://govloans.gov/govloans/
"Five federal agencies—U.S. Department of Agriculture, U.S. Department of Education, U.S. Department of Housing and Urban Development, U.S. Small Business Administration, and the U.S. Department of Veterans Affairs—have come together to create this single point of access for federal loan information on the Web." Browse or search for loans for farming, businesses, students, disaster relief, and more.

Grants.gov: Current Federal Funding Opportunities for Business and Commerce
http://www.grants.gov/FindGrantOpportunities

Grants.gov: Current Federal Funding Opportunities for Employment and Labor
http://www.grants.gov/FindGrantOpportunities

Idea Cafe's BizGrants
Idea Cafe's Guide to Government Grants
http://www.businessownersideacafe.com/business_grants/government_grants.html

Idea Cafe's Financing Your Biz
http://www.businessownersideacafe.com/financing/index.html
Idea Cafe's Feast of Financing : 40+ Pages of Tips and Tools to Help You Get the
Money Your Business Needs.

Landing A Business Loan
http://www.staples.com/content/article/i-n/landingabusinessloan.asp

Lesko's Business Help
http://www.lesko.com/help/BusinessHelp.htm
Money, information and services to start or expand a business.

MeL Entrepreneurial/Venture Capital Resources
http://mel.org/viewtopic.jsp?id=729&pathid=1382

Money for a Small Business
http://usgovinfo.about.com/library/weekly/blsba.htm
Think SBA loans, not grants. The About.Com web page also provides additional
advice.

National Association of Seed and Venture Capital Funds
http://www.nasvf.org/
The National Association of Seed and Venture Funds is an organization of private, public and nonprofit organizations committed to building their local
economies by investing and facilitating investment in local entrepreneurs.

Rural Information Center
Small Business Funding Resources
http://www.nal.usda.gov/ric/faqs/busnsfaq.htm
(Last checked 04/14/04)

Rural Information Center
Small Farm Funding Resources
http://www.nal.usda.gov/ric/faqs/farmfaq.htm

Small Business Administration
Financing Your Business
http://www.sba.gov/financing/
Describes the various loan programs of the U.S. Small Business Administration.

Small Business Administration
Microloan Program
http://www.sba.gov/financing/sbaloan/microloans.html
(Last checked 04/14/04)

Small Business Administration
Minority and Women's Prequalification Pilot Loan Program
http://www.sba.gov/business_finances/prequal/

Small Business Administration
Office of Women's Business Ownership
http://www.sbaonline.sba.gov/financing/special/women.html
Describes the many services and resources available for helping women succeed in business. Includes information on lending programs and venture capital.

Small Business Administration
Resources for Nonprofit Organizations
http://www.sbaonline.sba.gov/nonprofit/
This new area of SBA's web site is designed to help nonprofit organizations by presenting nonprofit information pertinent to small businesses, as well as to providing access to online Federal information and services.

State Small Business Grants
http://usgovinfo.about.com/library/weekly/blstategrants.htm
About.com provides a list of contact agencies in each state.

Tech Foundation Tech Grants
http://www.techfoundation.org/
Got a great skill or idea and just need some funding to launch your project? Visit this corporate technology funding site that helps the little guy make it big.

U.S. State and Local Gateway
Communities/Commerce Funding Opportunities
http://www.statelocal.gov/cdc-sub.html
A guide to funding opportunities, primarily federal grant programs.

Wall Street Journal Startup Journal Financing Information
http://www.startupjournal.com/financing/

GRANTS FOR NONPROFITS

HOMELESS

Capital Area District Library
Social Services Networking Links
http://www.cadl.org/local_links/SS.htm
Identifies local service agencies dealing with children and parenting, domestic abuse, emergency shelter and food, and other services.

Capital Area Emergency Services and Shelters
http://comnet.org/tcoa/emergenc.htm#header
A directory of local agencies providing emergency services and shelters, including:

☐ Adult Protective Services (Family Independence Agency)
☐ Advent House Ministries
☐ Board of Water and Light
☐ City Rescue Mission
☐ Council Against Domestic Assault
☐ Crisis Services for the Elderly
☐ Family Violence Prevention Helpline
☐ Grand Ledge Emergency Assistance Program
☐ Haven House
☐ Harvest House
☐ Lifeline
☐ Loaves and Fishes
☐ Medicall
☐ New Hope Center
☐ Relief After Violent Encounter, Inc. (RAVE)
☐ Seventh Day Adventists Community Services Food and Clothing Bank
☐ Stockbridge Community Outreach
☐ Volunteers of America

Emergency and Crisis Assistance from the U.S. Government
http://www.cfda.gov/public/grantsubtopic.asp?catcode=N#JMP3
Courtesy of the Catalog of Federal Domestic Assistance.

Emergency Food and Shelter National Board Program
http://www.efsp.unitedway.org/
The Emergency Food and Shelter National Board Program was created in 1983 to supplement the work of local social service organizations within the United States, both private and governmental, to help people in need of emergency assistance. This collaborative effort between the private and public sectors has disbursed over $2 billion in Federal funds during its 19-year history.

Evangelical Lutheran Church in America
Domestic Hunger Program
http://www.elca.org/grantinghope/
The Evangelical Lutheran Church in America Domestic Hunger Program provides assistance to fight hunger throughout the United States. Nonprofit organizations including ecumenical, inter-agency, or secular community groups are eligible to apply.

Helping The Homeless: Sample Fundraising Site
http://www.visionsacred.org

Homeless Facilities Grants
http://www.michigan.gov/mshda/0,1607,7-141—34606—,00.html
Agencies serving homeless populations may apply for Homeless Facilities Grants—generally not to exceed $50,000—for acquisition, rehabilitation, and new construction of facilities providing emergency shelter, transitional housing, permanent supportive housig, or directly associated supportive services. Applicants must provide dollar-for-dollar matching funds. Applications may be submitted at any time during the calendar year.

Mickey's Place in the Sun
Housing and Homelessness Resources
http://mickeys-place-in-the-sun.com/housing.html#Housing%20Finance
Find out where you can go for housing-related assistance. Contains info on clearinghouses, fair housing, downpayment resources, rural housing, federal and state government resources, homelessness, and more.

Newman's Own Charitable Foundation
http://www.newmansown.com/5_good.html
Offers grants to nonprofits, schools, hospitals, and other 501(c)(3) public benefit organizations. Eligible grant categories include: the arts, children and youth, health, education, the elderly, environment, the handicapped, literacy, substance abuse education, programs for the needy including housing and food, but no funding for individuals or scholarships.

Rural Assistance Center
Housing and Homelessness Funding
http://www.raconline.org/info_guides/housing/index.php

Top Ten U.S. Foundations Awarding Grants for Housing and Shelter, 2001
http://fdncenter.org/fc_stats/pdf/04_fund_sub/2001/50_found_sub/f_sub_1_01.pdf

U.S. Department of Housing and Urban Development
Office of Community Planning and Development
Homeless Assistance
http://www.hud.gov/offices/cpd/homeless/index.cfm
http://www.hud.gov/offices/cpd/homeless/programs/index.cfm
Homelessness is a problem that affects many people in America. If you are homeless yourself and need help or if you want to learn more about homelessness and how you can help, we have information for you. You can also find detailed information on HUD's homeless assistance programs on this web page.

GRANTS FOR NONPROFITS

HOUSING

Advent House Ministries' Home Buyer's Club
http://www.adventhouse.com/about.html
The Home Buyer's Club, which started in April 1997, teaches participants how to budget their money for monthly bills and then gives them an incentive to save toward a down payment on a house. For every $1 participants save, the program matches with $2—up to $4000. To qualify, participants must work at least 20 hours a week and make less than 80 percent of the HUD median income. For more information, call (517) 485-4722.

AmeriDream Inc.
http://www.ameridream.org/
Through down payment assistance and community redevelopment programs, AmeriDream, Inc. expands affordable housing opportunities not only to first-time homebuyers but to all low- and moderate-income individuals and families who wish to achieve homeownership.

Emergency Shelter Grants
http://www.michigan.gov/mshda/0,1607,7-141--34609--,00.html
Emergency Shelter Grants (ESG) are awarded to programs providing emergency shelter, transitional housing, and/or related supportive services for homeless individuals and/or families.

Enterprize Zones/Enterprise Communities (EZ/EC)
http://www.ezec.gov/
Provides information on the federal EZ/EC program as well as information on projects grantees. Sponsored by USDA and HUD. Includes recent grant opportunities in the areas of housing, public safety, jobs/job training, technology, research and development, education, youth, health, and environment.

Fannie Mae Foundation
http://www.fanniemaefoundation.org
The Fannie Mae Foundation has comprehensive nationwide grantmaking programs with a focus on supporting affordable homeownership and rental housing opportunities and community development.

Federal Funding Opportunities for Housing Posted on Grants.gov
http://www.grants.gov/FindGrantOpportunities
Lists some of the most recent grant programs available.

Federal Rer.t Assistance
http://www.hud.gov/renting/index.cfm
Describes assistance programs sponsored by the U.S. Department of Housing and Urban Development.

Fixing Up a Home and How to Finance It
http://www.pueblo.gsa.gov/cic_text/housing/fixhome/fixhome.htm

FreddieMac Foundation
http://www.freddiemacfoundation.org/core/grants/
Will continue to support programs that focus on the important work of preventing child abuse and neglect and finding permanent homes for children in foster care.

Grants.gov : Current Federal Funding Opportunities for Housing
http://www.grants.gov/FindGrantOpportunities

Home Depot Foundation
http://www.homedepotfoundation.org/
The Home Depot Foundation invests in nonprofit organizations throughout the United States and Canada that have demonstrated success within one of the grant-making initiatives of the Foundation. Through our investments, we support organizations and programs that work to:

☐ Create or rehabilitate affordable housing
☐ Assist at-risk youth (ages 12-18)
☐ Protect the environment
☐ Prepare for disasters

HOPE Awards
http://hopeawards.org/HopeAwrd.nsf/pages/categories?OpenDocument

Organizations and individuals making outstanding contributions to promote minority home ownership are invited to submit applications for the 2005 HOPE (Home Ownership Participation for Everyone) Awards. Each of the award winners in as many as seven categories will receive a $10,000 honorarium and national recognition for their contributions to removing barriers to minority home ownership.

Housing Assistance Council Development Loan Fund
http://www.ruralhome.org/loanfund/index.htm
The Housing Assistance Council operates one of the oldest community development loan funds in the country. HAC provides low-interest loans to finance affordable and mixed-income housing projects in rural communities nationwide. Loans are available to support projects at all stages in the development process, from predevelopment through construction.

Housing Grants Available from the State of Michigan
See State of Michigan Grants : Housing

Housing Grants Available from the U.S. Government
Posted on the Catalog of Federal Domestic Assistance
http://www.cfda.gov/public/grantsubtopic.asp?catcode=M
Subcategories include: Property and Mortgage Insurance, Homebuying, Homeownership, Home Improvement, Cooperatives, Rental, Rural Housing, Multifamily, Experimental and Development Projects, Indian Housing, Construction Rehabilitation, Planning, Land Acquisition, and Site Preparation for Housing.

Housing Grants/Programs from the U.S. Government
Posted on Grants.gov
http://www.grants.gov/FindGrantOpportunities
Some of the most current grant opportunities posted by the federal government.

HUD 203(k) Loan Program
http://usgovinfo.about.com/cs/consumer/a/fixeruppers.htm
You want to buy a house that needs repairs—a "fixer-upper." Unfortunately, you cannot borrow the money to buy the house, because the bank won't make the loan until the repairs are done, and the repairs cannot be done until the house has been purchased. Can you say "Catch-22?" Don't give up. The Department of Housing and Urban Development (HUD) has a loan program that might just get you that house. HUD's 203(k) program can help you with this quagmire and

allow you to purchase or refinance a property plus include in the loan the cost of making the repairs and improvements. The FHA insured 203(k) loan is provided through approved mortgage lenders nationwide. It is available to persons wanting to occupy the home. The downpayment requirement for an owner-occupant (or a nonprofit organization or government agency) is approximately 3 percent of the acquisition and repair costs of the property.

HUD Funding Opportunities
http://www.hud.gov/fundopp.html
A collection of web links to both government and private assistance programs compiled by the U.S. Department of Housing and Urban Development.

Lesko's Housing Help (Matthew)
http://www.lesko.com/help/HousingHelp.htm
Money, information and services to find, buy, or fix-up a home.

Neighborhood Reinvestment Corporation
http://www.nw.org/network/Home.asp
NeighborWorks is a national network of more than 220 community development and affordable housing organizations. The Neighborhood Reinvestment Corporation, created by Congress in 1978, provides training, grants, and technical support to the NeighborWorks network.

Partners in Charity
http://www.mortgagepages.com/pic/
PIC is a non-profit organization dedicated to helping you become a homeowner. Our mission is to gift downpayments to qualified buyers and help the community as a result. PIC provides a downpayment with no repayment and no second mortgage or lien of any type. It is a true gift to you!

Retirement Housing Organization
http://www.rhf.org/
RHF is one of the nation's largest non-profit providers of housing and services for the elderly, persons with disabilities, and low-income families.

Rural Assistance Center
Housing and Homelessness Funding
http://www.raconline.org/info_guides/housing/index.php

Rural Information Center
Housing Financing Options for Rural Areas
http://www.nal.usda.gov/ric/faqs/faqfront.htm

Top Ten U.S. Foundations Awarding Grants for Housing and Shelter, 2001
http://fdncenter.org/fc_stats/pdf/04_fund_sub/2001/50_found_sub/f_sub_1_01.pdf
Source: FC Stats.

U.S. Department of Housing and Urban Development
Office of Community Planning and Development
Affordable Housing
http://www.hud.gov/offices/cpd/affordablehousing/index.cfm
http://www.hud.gov/offices/cpd/affordablehousing/programs/index.cfm

GRANTS FOR NONPROFITS

HEALTH

AETNA Quality of Care Grants
http://www.aetna.com/foundation/news/articles/2004/pr_20040615.htm
$1 million available for racial and ethnic disparities and health end-of-life care programs.

Air Care Alliance
http://www.aircareall.org/
The Air Care Alliance is a nationwide organization of those pilots who volunteer to fly to provide assistance for health care, patient transportation or other volunteer missions. The website provides a listing of programs providing medical transportation, non-patient transports, and ways to volunteer. To locate information on the program near you, contact Air Care Alliance, 6202 South Lewis Ave., Suite F2, Tulsa, OK 74136; telephone: 918-745-0384 or 888-260-9707.

AirLifeLine
www.airlifeline.org
AirLifeLine is a national non-profit charitable organization of over 1,500 private pilots who fly ambulatory patients who cannot afford the cost of air travel to medical facilities for diagnosis and treatment. Participating pilots donate their time, aircraft and fuel to make this air transportation service totally free of charge for patients who qualify. Contact AirLifeLine National Office, 50 Fullerton Court # 200, Sacramento, CA 95825; telephone: 800-446-1231; 916-641-7800.

American Academy of Facial Plastic and Reconstructive Surgery
Face to Face Program
http://www.aafprs.org/media/humanitarian/m_humprog.html
FACE TO FACE, founded 1992, is a humanitarian and educational surgical exchange program conducted under the sponsorship of the Educational and Research Foundation for the American Academy of Facial Plastic and

Reconstructive Surgery (AAFPRS). In the United States and abroad, AAFPRS surgeons provide complimentary care to those who suffer from facial deformities caused by birth or trauma. The FACE TO FACE program offers individuals the opportunity to overcome the physical limitations placed on them by circumstances beyond their control—deformities at birth, domestic violence, and war.

American Legacy Foundation
Small Innovative Grant Program
http://www.americanlegacy.org
The American Legacy Foundation is dedicated to building a world where young people reject tobacco and anyone can quit. The Foundation provides Small Innovative Grants in order to advance innovative, evidence-based solutions to undo the harm from tobacco use in America.

Capital Assistance Funding :
A Rural Health Resource Guide
http://www.nal.usda.gov/ric/richspub/capasist.htm
Looking for funds to expand or renovate a building, purchase major equipment or construct a new facility can be challenging for a rural health provider. This guide is designed to help hospitals, clinics, community health centers, and other rural health providers learn more about various funding options to meet their capital needs.

Federal Funding Opportunities for Health Posted on Grants.gov
http://www.grants.gov/FindGrantOpportunities
Lists some of the most recent grant programs available.

Free Wheelchairs

☐ American Cancer Society, Inc., 1599 Clifton Road, NE, Atlanta, GA 30329; 800-ACS-2345.
☐ Easter Seals, 230 West Monroe Street, Suite 1800, Chicago, IL 60606; 800-221-6825; 312-726-6200; fax: 312-726-1494.
Easter Seals, the American Cancer Society and other helpful organizations provide free wheelchairs and other medical related equipment, like walkers, commodes, bathtub rails, bathtub chairs, crutches, transfer benches, electric wheelchairs and scooters, on a short-or long-term basis.

Funders Network Grantmakers Directory
Grantmakers that Address Adolescent Reproductive Health
http://web.archive.org/web/20010817133300/http://fundersnet.org/grants/adolescent.html

Funders Network Grantmakers Directory
Grantmakers that Address Reproductive Health Technologies
http://web.archive.org/web/20010817135645/http://fundersnet.org/grants/tech.html

Funders Network Grantmakers Directory
Grantmakers that Address Reproductive Rights and Access to Abortion
http://web.archive.org/web/20010309055934/http://www.fundersnet.org/grants/rights.html

FundsNet : Health Programs : Grantmaking Foundations
http://www.fundsnetservices.com/health2.htm
A collection of web links by FundsNet.

Gates Foundation (Bill and Melinda)
http://www.gatesfoundation.org/
Bill and Melinda Gates hope to make an enduring contribution toward increasing access to innovations in education, technology, and global health. More than seventeen billion dollars in endowments have been set aside for these causes.

Genentech Access to Health Care Foundation
http://www.gene.com/gene/about/corporate/uninsured-prog.jsp
Although Genentech's products are covered by most government and private insurance, Genentech has established the Access to Care Foundation for each of its marketed products to make them available to qualified uninsured or underinsured patients in the United States. A separate program covers medicine for cystic fibrosis.

Grants.gov : Current Federal Funding Opportunities for Health Issues
http://www.grants.gov/FindGrantOpportunities

Health Grants Available from the U.S. Government
Posted on the Catalog of Federal Domestic Assistance
http://www.cfda.gov/public/grantsubtopic.asp?catcode=L
Subcategories include: Alcoholism, Drug Abuse, and Mental Health—General, Alcoholism, Drug Abuse, and Mental Health—Law Enforcement, Alcoholism, Drug Abuse, and Mental Health—Planning, Alcoholism, Drug Abuse, and

Mental Health—Research, Communicable Diseases, Education and Training, Facility Loans and Insurance, Facility Planning and Construction, General Health and Medical, Health Research—General, Health Services Planning and Technical Assistance, Indian Health, Libraries, Information and Education Services, Maternity, Infants, Children, Mental Health, Occupational Safety and Health, Physical Fitness, Prevention and Control, Program Development, Specialized Health Research and Training, and Veterans Health.

Health Grants/Programs from the U.S. Government
Posted on Grants.gov
http://www.grants.gov/FindGrantOpportunities
Some of the most current grant opportunities posted by the federal government. Note: Select health as funding activity category and click on the search button at the bottom of the form.

Independent Charities of America
http://www.independentcharities.org/
Provides an interesting collection of medically-oriented operating foundations and agencies (among other focus areas) that conduct research on diseases such as AIDS, cancer, and glaucoma—just to name a few.

Johnson & Johnson Community Health Care Initiative
http://www.jhsph.edu/johnsonandjohnson
Johnson & Johnson Community Health Care Program, in partnership with the National Council of La Raza and Johns Hopkins Bloomberg School of Public Health, is pleased to announce a grant-funding opportunity for non-profit, community-based, health care organizations. The goal of the program is to assist community-based, nonprofit organizations whose primary goal is to provide creative and effective access to quality health care for the medically underserved.

Robert Wood Johnson Foundation
Local Initiative Funding Partners Program
http://www.rwjf.org/applying/cfpDetail.jsp?cfpCode=LFP&type=open
LIFP provides grants of $100,000 to $500,000 per project, which must be matched dollar-for-dollar by local grantmakers. The total award is paid out over a three- or four-year period. In 2005, up to $7.5 million will be awarded. For more information, eligibility requirements, and detailed application guidelines, visit www.rwjf.org/cfp/lifp.

Kresge Foundation Challenge Grants
http://www.kresge.org/programs/
A challenge grant program to upgrade and endow scientific instrumentation and laboratories in colleges and universities, teaching hospitals, medical schools, and research institutions. The minimum Kresge grant is $100,000 and the maximum is $500,000.

The Medicine Program
www.themedicineprogram.com
Free prescription medicine is available to any US citizen, of any age, who lacks insurance or has met their insurance limit. The Medicine Program was established to help patients who cannot afford necessary prescription drugs. You must be able to demonstrate your financial need. Contact The Medicine Program, P.O. Box 515, Doniphan, MO 63935; Telephone: 573-996-7300

Office of Rural Health Policy
Funding Opportunities
http://ruralhealth.hrsa.gov/funding/

PatientTravel.org
http://www.patienttravel.org/
The National Patient Travel Helpline provides information about all forms of charitable, long-distance medical air transportation and provides referrals to all appropriate sources of help available in the national charitable medical air transportation network.

Rural Assistance Center
Dental Health Funding
http://www.raconline.org/info_guides/dental/index.php

Rural Assistance Center
Emergency Medical Services Funding
http://www.raconline.org/info_guides/ems/index.html

Rural Assistance Center
Grant Funding Resources
http://www.raconline.org/info_guides/funding/index.html
http://www.raconline.org/funding/index.php
Identifies both government and non-government funding sources for rural health facilities.

Rural Health Services Funding : A Resource Guide
http://www.nal.usda.gov/ric/ricpubs/healthguide.htm
Compiled by Beth Blevins and Susan Marder, September

Rural Information Center Health Service (RICHS) Funding Resource
http://www.nal.usda.gov/ric/richs/funding.htm

Shrine of North America
http://www.shrinershq.org/
Support Shriners Hospitals for Children around the country that provide expert, no-cost orthopaedic and burn care to children under 18. For more information, contact Shriners Hospitals, P.O. Box 31356, Tampa, FL 33631; Telephone: 800-237-5055.

Small World Foundation
http://www.smallworld.org/
SWF is dedicated to providing reconstructive surgery and medical aid throughout the developing world for children and adults who have no access to proper health care or resources for treatment.

The Smile Train
http://www.smiletrain.org/
Treatment Grants are one-time grants for medical professionals, hospitals, and organizations that provide treatment for poor children with clefts in developing countries, but who may not meet the requirements to become a treatment partner. These grants are designed to supplement care for children who would not otherwise receive help through free treatment (i.e. surgery, orthodontia, speech therapy), improving the quality of treatment or providing for related expenses such as equipment, outreach programs, and patient travel.

Top 50 U.S. Foundations Awarding Grants for Mental Health, 2001
http://fdncenter.org/fc_stats/pdf/04_fund_sub/2001/50_found_sub/f_sub_f_01.pdf

Top 50 U.S. Foundations Awarding Grants for Public Health, 2001
http://fdncenter.org/fc_stats/pdf/04_fund_sub/2001/50_found_sub/f_sub_e70_01.pdf

Top 50 U.S. Foundations Awarding Grants for Reproductive Health, 2001
http://fdncenter.org/fc_stats/pdf/04_fund_sub/2001/50_found_sub/f_sub_e40_01.pdf
Source: FC Stats.

Traina Foundation (Nick)
http://www.nicktrainafoundation.org/main.htm
The Nick Traina Foundation was founded in 1998 by best-selling author Danielle Steel as a legacy to her son who lost his life to manic-depression. The Foundation supports organizations involved in the diagnosis, research, treatment, and/or family support of manic-depression, suicide prevention, child abuse and children in jeopardy.

Volunteer Pilots Association
http://www.volunteerpilots.org/
The Volunteer Pilots Association is a charitable non-profit organization providing air transportation to needy people who must travel to obtain medical treatment. Contact Volunteer Pilots Association, P.O. Box 471, Bridgeville, PA 15017; telephone: 412-221-1374; Email: info@volunteerpilots.org.

Volunteers in Health Care
http://volunteersinhealthcare.org/home.htm
A nationwide, nonprofit clearinghouse program established in 1997 as a resource for health care providers looking to organize or expand volunteer-led medical and dental services for the uninsured. Funded by the Robert Wood Johnson Foundation. Includes breaking news, grant info, etc.

GRANTS FOR NONPROFITS

MINORITIES

African American Foundations
http://www.cdsfunds.com/african-american_foundations.html
A list of web links provided by Custom Development Solutions, Inc., a consulting firm located in Isle of Palms, S.C.

Bubel Aiken Foundation (Disabilities)
http://www.bubelaikenfoundation.org/guidelines.htm
Clay Aiken's foundation for children with developmental disabilities announced a new partnership with Krispy Kreme Doughnuts, Inc. The new program will utilize Krispy Kreme fundraising programs across the United States to raise important funds for the Bubel/Aiken Foundation, which serves to bridge the gap that exists for young people with developmental disabilities.

Christopher Reeve Paralysis Foundation (Disabilities)
http://www.christopherreeve.org/
The Christopher Reeve Paralysis Foundation provides Quality of Life Grants to organizations nationwide that help improve opportunities, access and day-to-day quality of life for individuals living with disabilities, primarily paralysis, and their families. Grants support nonprofit organizations that address the needs of persons living with spinal cord injuries, their families and caregivers in twelve categories: children, arts, sports and recreation, education, advocacy, accessibility, practical service, independent living, assistive technology, therapeutic riding, employment and counseling. The Program also offers health promotion awards to nonprofit organizations that address paralysis caused by spinal cord injuries and other injuries, diseases and birth defects, including stroke, spina bifida, multiple sclerosis, cerebral palsy and amyotrophic lateral sclerosis. Nonprofit organizations throughout the United States, as well as internationally, are eligible to apply.

Mitsubishi Electric America Foundation (Disabilities)
http://www.meaf.org/grants/
The Mitsubishi Electric America Foundation matches employee contributions to nonprofit organizations which work with children with disabilities as well as providing direct grants to nonprofits who work with children with disabilities.

Soroptimist Midwest Grants
http://www.soroptimistmidwest.org/
Each year, the Soroptimist Foundation awards about $250,000 in Making a Difference for Women grants to more than 40 Soroptimist clubs that are initiating or continuing innovative projects that benefit women and girls. Sample projects include refurbishing domestic violence shelters, providing job training for women in transition, financing legal services for low-income women, providing mammograms to women with no health insurance, and sponsoring enrichment programs for at-risk girls. Clubs can receive awards between $500 and $10,000.

Special Needs/Disabilities Foundations
http://www.cdsfunds.com/special_needsdisabilities_foundations.html
Courtesy of the fund-raising firm Custom Development Solutions (CDS), 1470 Ben Sawyer Blvd., Ste 3, Mt. Pleasant, SC 29464; Toll Free: (800) 761-3833.

Third Wave Foundation
http://www.thirdwavefoundation.org/grants.html
The Organizing and Advocacy Fund of the Third Wave Foundation financially supports work, organizing and activism that exists to challenge sexism, racism, homophobia, economic injustice and other forms of oppression including projects that complement our other focus areas—reproductive rights and scholarships. We provide grants for specific projects and for general operating support.

ThreeHoops.com
http://threehoops.com/power/funds-other.htmlhttp://threehoops.com/power/funds-other.html
Lists private foundations that support Indian projects.

Women Related Foundations
http://www.cdsfunds.com/women-related_foundations.html
A compilation of web links by a fundr-raising firm Custom Development Solutions (CDS), 1470 Ben Sawyer Blvd., Ste 3, Mt. Pleasant, SC 29464; Toll Free: (800) 761-3833.

GRANTS FOR NONPROFITS

THE DISABLED

Alexander Graham Bell Association for the Deaf
http://www.agbell.org/financialaid.cfm
If your child is under 6 and has a moderate to profound hearing loss, you can apply for money to pay for intervention, educational and/or rehabilitation services. There is also money available for children with hearing loss between the ages of 5 and 19 to attend art or science courses during the summer, weekends, or even after school. For more information, contact: Alexander Graham Bell Association for the Deaf, 3417 Volta Place, NW, Washington, DC 20007; Telephone: 202-337-5220, TTY: 202-337-5221.

AMBUCS Therapeutic Tricycles for Disabled Children
http://www.ambucs.com/

American Academy of Allergy
http://www.aaaai.org/members/associates/asthmascholarship/default.stm
Associates to the American Academy of Allergy present at least 18 Award of Excellence Asthma Scholarships to graduating high school seniors with asthma. Scholarship monies may be used or applied only to pay for tuition, books and fees for a bona fide course of instruction at an accredited two-year or four-year college or university or accredited technical or vocational college or school.

American Council of the Blind
http://www.acb.org/
Student must be legally blind and a U.S. citizen or resident alien. Approximately twelve scholarships are awarded per year ranging from $1,000 to $5,000 each.

American Foundation for the Blind, Inc.
http://www.afb.org/

Association for Education and Rehabilitation of the Blind and Visually Impaired
William & Dorothy Ferrell Scholarship
http://www.aerbvi.org/modules.php?name=Content&pa=showpage&pid=77

Association of Blind Citizens
Assistive Technology Matching Grants
http://www.blindcitizens.org/assistive.html
The Association of Blind Citizens has established the Assistive Technology Fund.
The Assistive Technology Fund (ATF) will provide funds to cover 50% of the
retail price of adaptive devices or software.

Billy Barty Foundation
http://www.rth.org/bbf/
Sponsors a scholarship fund to help promising college students who have a medical form of dwarfism. Provides $2,000 scholarships.

Blinded Veterans Association
Kathern F. Gruber Scholarship Program
http://www.bva.org/services.html
Since the early '80s, BVA has offered spouses and dependent children of blinded
veterans a chance to continue their education through the Kathern F. Gruber
Scholarship Program.

Casey Martin Award
http://www.nike.com/nikebiz/nikebiz.jhtml?page=26&item=award&subitem=criteria

Christian Record Services Scholarships
http://www.christianrecord.org/site/services/scholarships.php
Partial scholarships are offered to legally blind young people striving to obtain a
college education.

Christine H. Eide Memorial Scholarship Award
http://www.lighthouse.org/eide_scholarship.htm
In memory of his daughter, Torris Eide of Queens, New York established this award
for students who are legally blind. The scholarship is available to full-time students
to full-time students entering or attending an accredited college or university.

Cystic Fibrosis Scholarship Foundation (CFSF)
http://www.cfscholarship.org/

The mission of the Cystic Fibrosis Scholarship Foundation (CFSF) is to provide an opportunity for young adults with CF to further their education at a college or vocational school.

Disabled and Handicapped Services Grants from the U.S. Government
http://www.cfda.gov/public/grantsubtopic.asp?catcode=N#JMP1

DisabilityInfo.gov
http://www.disabilityinfo.gov/
New federal website that is a portal to federal and federally funded programs and services.

Disability Resources Monthly Guide to Disability Resources on the Internet
http://www.disabilityresources.org/
Includes links to financial aid and grants resources.

Ethel Louise Armstrong Foundation (ELA)
http://www.ela.org
Supports professional organizations that work with people with disabilities through grants and scholarships that further their goals of education, advocacy, leadership development, mentorship and the arts.Grants are small, ranging from $1,000 to $5,000. For more information contact Ms. Deborah Lewis, 626-398-8840, email: executive director@ela.org.

Financial Aid for Eye Care
http://www.nei.nih.gov/health/financialaid.htm
The National Eye Institute provides a directory of possible program assistance.

Financial Aid for Students With Disabilities
http://www.parentsinc.org/finaid/finaid.html
This list contains sources of financial aid where a primary criteria is that the student experience a disability.

Guide Dog Foundation for the Blind, Inc
http://www.guidedog.org
This charity provides trained guide dogs to the blind at absolutely no charge. They also include training in using the dog and will pay for room and board, all equipment, and round trip transportation. For more information, contact: Guide Dog Foundation for the Blind, Inc, 371 East Jericho Tpke., Smithtown, NJ 11787; Telephone: 800-548-4337; 631-265-2121.

HEATH Resource Center
http://www.heath.gwu.edu/
George Washington University has received a grant from the U.S. Department of Education's Office of Special Education and Rehabilitative Services to operate the National Clearinghouse on Postsecondary Education for Individuals with Disabilities, known as the HEATH Resource Center. The web page contains information about funding opportunities along with many other resources.

Immune Deficiency Foundation Annual Scholarship Program
http://www.primaryimmune.org/services/scholarship.htm
The Immune Deficiency Foundation has awarded scholarships to undergraduate students living with a primary immune deficiency disease.

Joseph P. Kennedy Jr Foundation
http://www.jpkf.org/
The Joseph P. Kennedy, Jr. Foundation, established in 1946 by Ambassador and Mrs. Joseph P. Kennedy, honors their eldest son who was killed in World War II. The Foundation has two major objectives: to improve the way society deals with its citizens who have mental retardation (intellectual disabilities), and to help identify and disseminate ways to prevent the causes of mental retardation (intellectual disabilities).

Lilly Reintegration Scholarship
http://zyprexa.com/reintegration/reintegration_scholarship.html
The goal of the Lilly Reintegration Scholarship is to help people with schizophrenia and related schizophrenia-spectrum disorders to acquire the educational and vocational skills necessary to reintegrate into society, secure jobs and regain their lives.

Kurzwell Educational Systems
Teacher Resources—Funding Information Sources for Assistive Technology
http://kurzweiledu.com/proof_resources_funding.asp

Lucent Pioneer Organization Scholarship
No URL: For more information, call 1-888-999-5877
The Lucent Pioneer Organization offers scholarships to assist with tuition for physically and mentally challenged students in pursuit of education.

Minnie Pearl Ear Foundation Scholarship
http://www.earfoundation.com/

Multiple Sclerosis Foundation
Brighter Tomorrow Grant Program
http://www.msfocus.org/programs_events/prog_grants_bwmg.html
The Multiple Sclerosis Foundation is a national nonprofit organization dedicated to enhancing the quality of life of those diagnosed with MS. The Brighter Tomorrow Grant is an award of up to $1,000 to provide goods or services that will help improve the quality of life of someone with MS.

National Organization on Disability : Housing Access
http://www.nod.org/housing/index.cfm

NEC Foundation of America
http://www.necfoundation.org/
Makes cash grants to nonprofit organizations and programs with national reach and impact in one or both of the following arenas: science and technology education, principally at the secondary level, and/or the application of technology to assist people with disabilities.

Opportunities for the Blind
http://www.opportunitiesfortheblind.org/info.htm
Assists U.S.A. citizens of working age who are legally blind. Funding is available for scholarships and training, self-employment projects, special equipment, and job related services. All prospective applicants must first submit an Eligibility Form or call 1-240-420-6500

Pfizer's Epilepsy Scholarship Award
http://www.epilepsy-scholarship.com/
One year $3000 award goes to 16 college students each year.

Pilot Dogs, Inc.
http://www.pilotdogs.org/
This charity gives its trained animals to the blind at absolutely no charge. They also include four weeks of training in using the dog and will pay for room and board, all equipment, and round trip transportation. For more information, contact: Pilot Dogs, Inc., 625 West Town Street, Columbus, OH 43215; Telephone: 614-221-6367; Fax: 614-221-1577

Special Needs/Disabilities Foundations
http://www.cdsfunds.com/special_needsdisabilities_foundations.html

United Cerebral Palsy (UCP) National Office
Grants and Contracts Office
http://www.ucp.org/ucp_general.cfm/1/6619

United Student Aid Funds
Access to Education Scholarship
http://www.usafunds.org/borrowers/access_to_education_scholarship.html
Provides $1,500 to students with an annual family income of less than $35,000.
Up to 50% of awards will be targeted to applicants who are members of an ethnic-minority group or who have a physical disability.

GRANTS FOR NONPROFITS

THE AGED

Administration on Aging
Grant Programs
http://www.aoa.gov/doingbus/doingbus.asp
Each year, Congress appropriates funds for use by AoA and the other Federal Agencies in carrying out their mission. AoA provides grant funding to States and territories, recognized Native American Tribes and Hawaiian Americans, as well as nonprofit organizations, including faith-based and academic institutions. Individuals are not eligible to apply for AoA funding.

Administration on Aging
More Internet Resources for Grant Seekers In Aging
http://www.aoa.gov/doingbus/more/more.asp

Alliance for Aging Research (AAR)
http://www.agingresearch.org/
This private, not-for-profit science policy advocacy organization administers funds for training and research in geriatrics.

Altria Group Corporate Contributions Program
The Senior Helpings Program
http://www.altria.com/responsibility/04_05_01_01_01_hungergrantprograms.asp
The Senior Helpings Program, an initiative of Altria Companies Inc. in partnership with the National Meals on Wheels Foundation, awards grants to nonprofit organizations across the country in order to expand and improve food and nutrition programs for homebound seniors. Grants of up to $25,000 are awarded to meals-on-wheels service providers for the provision of meals to the homebound elderly. Nonprofit organizations throughout the United States are eligible to apply.

Alzheimer's Association (AA)
http://www.alz.org/
The Association provides funds for conferences and research.

American Geriatrics Society (AGS)
http://www.americangeriatrics.org/index.shtml
AGS is a not-for-profit organization of health care professionals in the field of geriatrics.

American Health Assistance Foundation (AHAF)
http://www.ahaf.org/
A nonprofit charitable organization with over 25 years dedicated to: (1) Funding research on Alzheimer's disease, glaucoma, macular degeneration, heart disease, and stroke, (2) Educating the public about these diseases, and (3) Providing emergency financial assistance to Alzheimer's disease patients and their caregivers.

American Health Assistance Foundation
Alzheimer's Family Relief Program
http://www.ahaf.org/afrp/afrp.htm
The American Health Assistance Foundation's Alzheimer's Family Relief Program (AFRP) provides direct financial assistance and resources for the continued care and support of Alzheimer's patients and their caregivers. Grants are provided for expenses such as short-term nursing care, home health care, respite care, adult day care, medications, medical or personal hygiene supplies, transportation, and other expenses related to care for the patient with Alzheimer's disease.

Commonwealth Fund
http://www.cmwf.org/
The Fund's current four national program areas are improving health care services, bettering the health of minority Americans, advancing the well-being of elderly people, and developing the capacities of children and young people.

HCR Manor Care Foundation
http://www.hcr-manorcare.org/
The mission of the HCR Manor Care Foundation is to enhance the quality of life in the communities served by HCR Manor Care through support of nonprofit organizations focused on improving the quality of life for seniors, individuals requiring post-acute services, and those needing hospice and palliative care.

HelpingPatients.Org
http://www.helpingpatients.org/index.cfm
This site was designed to help you find patient assistance programs for which you may qualify. This online service is free and completely confidential—we do not keep records of any personally identifiable information.

Johnson (Robert Wood) Faith in Action Program
http://www.fiavolunteers.org/
Faith in Action is a national volunteer movement that brings together religious congregations from many faiths and other community organizations. Their common mission is to help people who are aging and chronically ill maintain their independence by providing them assistance with everyday activities. The program will be giving $35,000 grants to 2,000 organizations in the next six years, plus technical assistance. They're looking for organizations that have five things: they're interfaith, they use volunteers, they provide caregiving services, to people with chronic health conditions, and the services are provided in people's homes. It's a $100 million program, one of the ten largest foundation grants ever, according to USA Today.

National Association of Area Agencies on Aging
http://www.n4a.org
Looking for the local meals on wheels programs or need a home health aide for mom? The Eldercare Locator searches their database for the services for seniors in any area of the country. These can include transportation, legal assistance, housing options, recreation and social activities, adult daycare, senior center programs, and more. Contact the Eldercare Locator, National Association of Area Agencies on Aging, 1112 16th St., NW, Washington, DC 20036; telephone: 800-677-1116 (9 a.m.- 8 p.m. EST).

Newman's Own Charitable Foundation
http://www.newmansown.com/5_good.html
Offers grants to nonprofits, schools, hospitals, and other 501(c)(3) public benefit organizations. Eligible grant categories include: the arts, children and youth, health, education, the elderly, environment, the handicapped, literacy, substance abuse education, programs for the needy including housing and food, but no funding for individuals or scholarships.

Old Age Assistance Grants Available from the U.S. Government
http://www.cfda.gov/public/grantsubtopic.asp?catcode=N#JMP9

Retirement Housing Organization
http://www.rhf.org/
RHF is one of the nation's largest non-profit providers of housing and services for the elderly, persons with disabilities, and low-income families.

Retirement Research Foundation
http://www.rrf.org/
The Retirement Research Foundation, based in Chicago, is the nation's largest private foundation exclusively devoted to aging and retirement issues. It makes approximately $8 million in grants each year to nonprofit and educational organizations to support programs, research and public policy studies to improve the quality of life of older Americans. It was created by the late John D. MacArthur.

Senior Related Foundations
http://www.cdsfunds.com/senior-related_foundations.html

GRANTS FOR NONPROFITS

RECREATION

Able to Play Initiative
http://www.abletoplay.org/

American Eagle Outfitters Foundation
AE RIDE National Skatepark Program
http://www.ae.com/corp/foundation.htm

Athletics/Sports Funding Opportunities Posted by the Foundation Center RFP Bulletin
http://fdncenter.org/pnd/rfp/cat_athletics.jhtml

Baseball Tomorrow Fund
http://www.mlb.com/NASApp/mlb/mlb/official_info/mlb_official_community_bbtomorrow.jsp
http://bigleaguers.yahoo.com/mlbpa/btf.html
The Baseball Tomorrow Fund is a joint initiative of Major League Baseball and the Major League Baseball Players Association. The mission of the Baseball Tomorrow Fund is to promote and enhance the growth of Baseball in the United States, Canada and throughout the world by funding programs, fields and equipment purchases, designed to encourage and maintain youth participation in the game. Grants from the Baseball Tomorrow Fund are designed to be sufficiently flexible to enable applicants to address needs unique to their communities. The funds may be used to finance a new program, expand or improve an existing program, undertake a new collaborative effort, or obtain facilities or equipment necessary for youth baseball or softball programs.

Bike Belong Coalition Grants
http://bikesbelong.org/site/page.cfm?PageID=21

Bikes Belong Coalition, whose mission is putting more people on bicycles more often, accepts requests for funding of up to $10,000 for facility, capacity, and education projects. Bikes Belong also accepts successor proposals from previously funded projects.

Bill Bowerman Track Renovation Program
http://www.nike.com/nikebiz/media/BowermanRFP.pdf
Nike provides up to $50,000 to nonprofit organizations to refurbish running tracks around the world.

Finish Line Youth Foundation
Youth Athletic and Wellness Programs Supported
http://www.finishline.com/store/corporate_info/youthfoundation.jsp
The Finish Line Youth Foundation provides funding to organizations in the communities in which company stores are located, or communities where donations to the Foundation are raised.

Funding a Park
http://www.skateparkguide.com/FUNDINGAPARK.htm
Practical advice on raising funds for a skateboard park from Anthony Gembeck, TransWorld Skateboard Business Magazine.

Galyan's Community Giving Program
http://www.galyans.com/news_frameset.html
Since 1946, Galyan's has supported nonprofit organizations, youth leagues, and community events in the communities they serve.

Hasbro Children's Foundation
http://www.hasbro.org
The mission of the Foundation is to improve the quality of life for disadvantaged children through age 12 by supporting innovative, model, direct-service programs in the areas of healthk education and social services. The Foundation also funds universally accessible play spaces. Most often, local grants for model community programs range from $500 to $35,000 each. For multi-site expansions, awards start at $35,000 and are granted over a period of one to three years. Priority will be given to economically disadvantaged areas for playground refurbishment and/or new construction. For more information, contact Hasbro Children's Foundation, 32 W. 23rd St., New York, NY 10010.
Also listed under Children and Youth.

Inner City Games Foundation
http://www.inner-citygames.org/
The mission of the Inner-City Games is to provide opportunities for inner-city youth to participate in sports, educational, cultural and community enrichment programs; to build confidence and self-esteem; to encourage youth to say "no" to gangs, drugs and violence and "yes" to hope, learning and life. Currently limited to Atlanta, Chicago, Columbus, Dallas, Detroit, Houston, Las Vegas, Los Angeles, New York, Orlando, Philadelphia, San Antonio, San Diego, San Jose, and Southern Florida.

Mia Hamm Foundation
http://www.miafoundation.org/
Provides funds for opportunities for women in sports and bone marrow research.

NFL Charities Youth Education, Recreation, and Physical Fitness Grants
NFL Charities, a nonprofit organization founded in 1973 by member clubs of the National Football League, awards grants in the following areas: youth education, recreation, and physical fitness (impact grants and partner grants); sports-related medical research; volunteer recreation programs (League-managed programs only); and NFL Player organizations. Through its grant programs, NFL Charities seeks to enhance the educational opportunities for school-age youth. Organizations applying for funding through this program may seek either an Impact Grant or a Partner Grant and must specify the type of grant on the proposal. Organizations may not apply for both types of grants in the same funding cycle.

Through its *Impact Grants*, NFL Charities seeks to support education, mentoring, or youth-centered programming that show potential for national impact. NFL Charities will support the program development, pilot, and implementation phases of school-based or youth agency-based projects. The ultimate goal is to fund the enhancement of existing systems or the creation of new initiatives to address the educational and recreational needs of school-aged youth on a national scope. NFL Charities is dedicated to encouraging children to stay in school, to achieve academically, and to participate in enriching after-school and recreational activities in order to promote their development into productive members of society. Major multi-year proposals will be considered, with a maximum of four years of funding. Each year of funding is contingent upon meeting grant requirements; grants over $250,000 may require a site visit. Grants will only be awarded to national nonprofit organizations defined as tax-exempt under Section 501(c)(3) of the IRS Code. No grants will be awarded to individuals.

Through its Partner Grants, NFL Charities seeks to support organizations with established strategic partnerships or previous grantmaking relationships with the

NFL. Partner grants will be awarded to organizations that focus on youth-centered educational and recreational programming. Grants typically range from $5,000 to $25,000. Multi-year grants will not be considered. Grants will only be awarded to national nonprofit organizations defined as tax-exempt under Section 501(c)(3) of the IRS Code. No grants will be awarded to individuals or individual schools.

Grant applications must be postmarked by August 1. Organizations will be notified by mail by the end of the calendar year about the status of grant proposals. To request application materials and/or inquire about the status of grant proposals, contact: Jessica Rich, NFL Charities, 280 Park Avenue, 17th Floor, New York, NY 10017; E-mail: richj@nfl.com.

NFL Grassroots Program
http://www.liscnet.org/whatwedo/programs/nfl/
The NFL Grassroots Program is a partnership of the National Football League (NFL) and the Local Initiatives Support Corporation (LISC) to provide nonprofit, neighborhood-based organizations with financing and technical assistance to improve the quality, safety, and accessibility of local football fields.

Parks and ball fields can serve as tremendous community assets because they offer opportunities for recreation, education, and relaxation that contribute to the local quality of life, especially for young people. In four years of programming, the Grassroots Program has awarded $6.3 million in grants for 71 projects with total development costs of $23 million in over 40 cities across the country.

Nickelodian's Lets Just Play Grant Program
http://www.nick.com/all_nick/everything_nick/public_ljpgrants2.jhtml
The "Lets Just Play" campaign by Nickelodeon will award a half-million dollars in grants to schools and after-school programs to provide resources to create and expand opportunities for physical play. Elementary schools, middle schools and after-school programs across the country are eligible to enter the grants program. The "Let's Just Play" campaign is a grassroots effort to get kids more physically active and to encourage more healthy lifestyles for kids across America. In addition to the grant, activities and events are to take place across the country to encourage positive play for America's youth.

Also listed under Children and Youth.

NRA Foundation
http://www.nrafoundation.org/
The NRA Foundation National and State Fund grants are focused on the following general categories: Youth Programs, Range Improvement and Development,

Public Safety, Education and Training, Wildlife and Natural Resource Conservation and Constitutional Research and Education.

Off the Course.Foundation
Also known as the Tiger Woods Foundation
http://ww1.sportsline.com/u/fans/celebrity/tiger/course/foundation.html
Sponsors golf clinics in major metropolitan areas in the U.S. for young people historically denied access and exposure to the sport, supporting programs that promote educational achievement and job opportunities for inner-city and other disadvantaged youth, and participate in programs and events that promote racial harmony and help people understand and appreciate the value of inclusiveness.

Potential Resources for Playground Safety Funding
http://www.uni.edu/playground/resources/funding.html
This web site, sponsored by the University of Northern Iowa National Program for Playground Safety, identifies funders who may assist in providing safer playground equipment for schools and other public facilities.

Recreation Grants Available from the State of Michigan,
http://www.lib.msu.edu/harris23/grants/staterec.htm

Recreation Grants Available from the U.S. Government
http://www.cfda.gov/public/grantsubtopic.asp?catcode=C#JMP5

RYKÄ Women's Fitness Grant
http://www.wfnet.org/news/story.php?story_id=167
The Women's Sports Foundation and RYKÄ have joined together to provide fitness grants to support organizations and individuals that enhance women's lives through health-and fitness-related programs. The RYKÄ Women's Fitness Grant, available to women aged 25 and over, will provide up to $50,000 in financial assistance. RYKÄ, an athletic footwear manufacturing company, is committed to enhancing women's lives through fitness. The RYKÄ Women's Fitness Grant is currently available via http://www.WomensSportsFoundation.org under the Funding section or by calling 800-227-3988.

Sports Charities and Foundations
http://www.usatoday.com/sports/2001-07-20-privatea.htm

Tiger Woods Foundation
Also known as Off the Course.Foundation
http://ww1.sportsline.com/u/fans/celebrity/tiger/course/foundation.html
Sponsors golf clinics in major metropolitan areas in the U.S. for young people historically denied access and exposure to the sport, supporting programs that promote educational achievement and job opportunities for inner-city and other disadvantaged youth, and participate in programs and events that promote racial harmony and help people understand and appreciate the value of inclusiveness.

Tony Hawks Foundation
http://www.tonyhawkfoundation.org/grant_images/grant.htm
http://www.skateboarding.com/skate/skate_biz/article/0,12364,266145,00.html
Established by professional skateboarder Tony Hawk, the nonprofit Tony Hawk Foundation works to promote high-quality, public skateparks in low-income areas throughout the United States. The second link is an article in Transworld Skatboarding Business about the Tony Hawks Foundation.

United States Handball Association
http://ushandball.org/html/dev_grant.html
Funding for youth handball projects…is available through the United States Handball Association. Any person or group interested in starting a handball program for youngsters may submit a proposal. Programs may be organized within school instruction, after-school programs, or community or club/Y programs. For more information contact: Vern Roberts, 520-795-0434, email: handball@ushandball.org.

United States Soccer Federation Foundation
http://www.ussoccerfoundation.org/
The United States Soccer Federation Foundation Inc., has established a new Web site to distribute grant application information nationally and provide the latest foundation news, including grant recipient profiles, annual reports, and director and officer profiles. Foundation Chairman James Hamilton says that in its first two years the foundation received hundreds of applications and awarded more than $4 million to 56 programs in 28 states. Grant applications, instructions and guidelines are available on the Web site or by mail by calling the foundation at (202) 496-1292. Average grants range from $10,000-$100,000. The site provides links to other soccer web sites as well.

USA Today's Sports Charities
http://www.usatoday.com/sports/2001-07-20-privatea.htm

USA TODAY identified more than 350 public charities and private foundations connected to professional athletes or teams. Newly formed charities, those operated by teams and those which appeared dormant were eliminated from the analysis to focus on established non-profit organizations founded by sports figures.

Women's Sports Foundation Funding Opportunities
http://www.womenssportsfoundation.org/cgi-bin/iowa/funding/index.html
The Women's Sports Foundation is a leading provider of funding and resources for grants and scholarships to girls and women in sports.

Women's Sports Foundation
http://www.womenssportsfoundation.org/cgi-bin/iowa/funding/results.htm
The Women's Sports Foundation (WSF) promotes the growth of women in sports leadership positions, especially in the areas of coaching, officiating, and sports administration.

Youth Recreation Grants for Homeless Program
http://www.toy-tia.org/industry/ATI/grant-guidelines.html
The Toy Industry Foundation provides grants for programs that enhance the healthy development of children living in homeless situations through play and recreation activities, through community outreach and collaboration. Priority is given to programs that serve as models for other organizations and lend themselves to measurable evaluation, with results that may be disseminated to wide audiences.
Also listed under Children.

GRANTS FOR NONPROFITS

LAW AND CRIMINAL JUSTICE

7-Eleven Community Outreach Programs
http://www.7-eleven.com/about/outreachprograms.asp
7-Eleven supports non-profits, libraries, and schools particularly in the following areas: (1) Education is our signature cause, specifically programs that assist adolescents and adults (ages 14 and above) with: Workforce Developmentand Language Education. 7-Eleven is especially interested in programs that assist at-risk and economically disadvantaged individuals. (2) The company also supports educational programs that recognize the rich cultural diversity in our communities and promote better understanding and tolerance among cultures throughout America. 7-Eleven has a specific interest in programs that serve ethnic and inner-city constituents. (3) 7-Eleven supports programs designed to prevent crime and build stronger, safer and more caring communities, with a special interest in youth-related programs. (4) 7-Eleven also supports the fight against hunger, providing by in-kind contributions of fresh foods to pre-selected food banks in markets where 7-Eleven operates.
Normal grants fall in the $1000-$2500 range and are not renewable.

American Bar Association Juvenile Justice Center
Non-Profits and Fundraising Web Links
http://www.abanet.org/crimjust/juvjus/linkprofit.html

American Probation and Parole Association
Grant Programs
http://www.appa-net.org/grant%20and%20special%20projects/grant.htm

Anti-Human Trafficking Funding Available
http://www.ojp.usdoj.gov/BJA/grant/HumanTraffic.html

Bulletproof Vest Partnership
http://www.vests.ojp.gov/
Funding program for state and local law enforcement agencies to acquire bullet-proof vests.

Byrne Memorial State and Local Law Enforcement Assistance (Edward)
http://www.ojp.usdoj.gov/BJA/grant/byrne.html
http://www.cfda.gov/public/viewprog.asp?progid=531
The Edward Byrne Memorial State and Local Law Enforcement Assistance Grant Program (Byrne Formula Grant Program) is a partnership among federal, state, and local governments to create safer communities. BJA is authorized to award grants to states for use by states and units of local government to improve the functioning of the criminal justice system—with emphasis on violent crime and serious offenders—and enforce state and local laws that establish offenses similar to those in the federal Controlled Substances Act (21 U.S.C. 802(6) et seq.).
Grants may be used to provide personnel, equipment, training, technical assistance, and information systems for more widespread apprehension, prosecution, adjudication, detention, and rehabilitation of offenders who violate such state and local laws. Grants also may be used to provide assistance (other than compensation) to victims of these offenders. Twenty-nine legislatively authorized purpose areas were established to define the nature and scope of programs and projects that may be funded under the Byrne Formula Grant Program.

Chief Corporation Public Safety Grants Consulting
http://www.chiefsupply.com/grants/

Community Oriented Policing Services (COPS) Funding Opportunities
http://www.cops.usdoj.gov/default.asp?Item=46
The U.S. Department of Justice Office of Community Oriented Policing Services (COPS) is seeking proposals to fund a variety of initiatives designed to enhance local law enforcement community policing efforts.

COPS in Schools Program Grants
http://www.usmayors.org/uscm/us_mayor_newspaper/documents/04_12_04/cops.asp
The Department of Justice Office of Community Oriented Policing Services (COPS) announces the availability of the COPS in Schools grant program, which will assist law enforcement agencies in hiring new, additional School Resource Officers (SROs) to engage in community policing in and around primary and secondary schools.

Drug-Free Communities Support Program Funds Now Available
http://ojjdp.ncjrs.org/dfcs/
OJJDP and ONDCP announce the availability of FY 2004 Drug- Free Communities Support Program funding. Approximately 180 grants of up to $100,000 each will be awarded to community coalitions working to prevent youth substance abuse. (OJJDP)

Federal Funding Opportunities for Law, Justice, and Legal Services Posted on Grants.gov
http://www.grants.gov/FindGrantOpportunities
Lists some of the most recent grant programs available.

Grants for High Tech Police Equipment
http://www.x20.org/thermal/LawEnforcement.htm
Provides a "helpful guide" for law enforcement Officials who are interested in writing "grant Proposals" to obtain specialized or high technology surveillance equipment for their respective departments.

Grants.gov : Current Federal Funding Opportunities for Consumer Protection
http://www.grants.gov/FindGrantOpportunities

Human Rights Foundations
http://www.cdsfunds.com/human-rights_foundations.html
Courtesy of the fund-raising firm Custom Development Solutions (CDS), 1470 Ben Sawyer Blvd., Ste 3, Mt. Pleasant, SC 29464; Toll Free: (800) 761-3833.

JustInfo
http://www.ncjrs.org/justinfo/dates.html
Often lists criminal justice funding opportunities for both nonprofits and indivduals.

Law, Justice, and Legal Studies Grants/Programs from the U.S. Government Posted on Grants.gov
http://www.grants.gov/FindGrantOpportunities
Some of the most current grant opportunities posted by the federal government.

Law, Justice, and Legal Services Grants from the U.S. Government
http://www.cfda.gov/public/grantsubtopic.asp?catcode=P

Minnesota Center Against Violence and Abuse (MINCAVA)
Electronic Clearinghouse
Funders Online
http://www.mincava.umn.edu/fol.asp

NCJRS Links to Justice Grants
http://www.ncjrs.org/fedgrant.html
A compilation of web links to U.S. Department of Justice agencies that fund researchers and practitioners engaging in specific criminal and juvenile justice projects.

Office for the Victims of Crimes
Discretionary Funding Opportunities
http://www.ojp.usdoj.gov/ovc/fund/dakit.htm

Office for the Victims of Crimes
Grants and Funding Opportunities
http://www.ojp.usdoj.gov/ovc/fund/welcome.html

Office for the Victims of Crimes
Professional Development Scholarships
http://www.ovcttac.org/scholarship.cfm
OVC announces the availability of Professional Development Scholarships for those who work with victims of crime. The program assists organizations with insufficient funds and covers training-related costs, including travel. Awards may be up to $1,000 for individuals and up to $5,000 for multidisciplinary teams. (OVC)

Office of Justice Programs
Funding Opportunities
http://www.ojp.usdoj.gov/fundopps.htm

Office of Justice Programs
Resource Guide
http://www.ojp.usdoj.gov/ResGuide/
This Resource Guide provides information on OJP activities and programs and highlights resources available for collaborative relationships with criminal justice and community organizations.

Office of National Drug Control Policy
Funding Opportunities
http://www.whitehousedrugpolicy.gov/funding/index.html

Public Welfare Foundation Criminal Justice Grants
http://www.publicwelfare.org/grants/criminal_justice.asp

Public Welfare Foundation Human Rights and Global Security Grants
http://www.publicwelfare.org/grants/human_rights_global_security.asp
Approximately $2.5 million is available.

Responding First to Bioterrorism : Federal Funding Opportunities
http://www.nap.edu/shelves/first/Funding.html

State Victim Clinic Program Grant Solicitation
http://www.lclark.edu/org/ncvli/2004grantapp.html
With OVC funding, the National Crime Victim Law Institute is seeking State
Victim Clinic Program Grant Solicitations for establishing crime victim legal
clinics to provide direct legal services to victims of felony and violent crimes.

State Funding for Homeland Security
http://www.nasbo.org/Publications/PDFs/state%20funding%20for%20security.pdf

Top 50 U.S. Foundations Awarding Grants for Civil Rights and Social Action, 2001
http://fdncenter.org/fc_stats/pdf/04_fund_sub/2001/50_found_sub/f_sub_r_01.pdf

GLOSSARY OF TERMS

GLOSSARY OF TERMS

Capital Request—A planned undertaking to purchase, build or renovate space or building or to acquire equipment

Community—The people living in the same district, city, state, etc.

Contribution—A tax-deductible gift, cash, property, equipment or services from an individual to a non-profit organization. Most often given annually.

General Operating Support—Funds, both contributions and grants, which support the ongoing services of the organization.

Grants—Generally an allocation from foundations, corporations, or government for special projects or general operating. May be multi-year or annual.

Indicator—The observable, measurable characteristic or change that represents achievement of the outcome.

In-Kind Support—A contribution of equipment/materials, time, and or services that the donor has placed a monetary value on for tax purposes.

Methodology—A sequence of activities needed to accomplish the program objectives.

Outcomes—The changes in, (or benefits achieved by) clients due to their participation in program activities. This may include changes to participants' knowledge, skills, values, behavior, or condition of status.

Performance Standard—The number and percent of clients who are expected to achieve the result. Also called target, they should be set based on professional judgment, past data, research, or professional standards.

Program—An organized set of services designed to achieve specific outcomes for a specified population that will continue beyond the grant period.

Project—A planned undertaking or organized set of services designed to achieve specific outcomes that begins and ends within the grant period. (a successful project may become an ongoing program)

Success Story—An example that illustrates your program's effect on a client.

OTHER BOOKS
BY ANTHONY HOLLIS

Everything you need to know about grants
By Anthony Hollis

This comprehensive step-by-step guide on grant seeking covers everything from understanding the funder, developing a fundable project to creating measurable goals and objectives, and writing a winning proposal. Examples, guide sheets, worksheets and more are included. It's a one-of-a-kind book with a level of detail not found elsewhere in the marketplace. This clear, step-by-step guide to locating grants and funding organizations delivers: An overview of what types of grants are available and how to apply for them. Strategies for cutting through red tape. A guide to the grant-writing terminology. An explanation of why some proposals succeed while others fail. Samples of successful grant proposals. A directory of resources critical to grant seekers. Includes Internet addresses of organizations publishing information about grant makers; Federal, Foundation, Corporation, State and Regional grants resources contact information. More than 2000 grant resources.

Anthony Hollis Secrets to Credit Repair
By Anthony Hollis

Solve your financial and credit problems once and for all! Anthony Hollis' Secrets to Credit Repair is a dynamic, easy—to—follow program. It outlines specific, jargon-free instructions on how to eliminate your debts, remove negative items from your credit files, and establish an AAA-1 credit rating—regardless of your past or present financial situation once and for all!

How to get a Business Loan or Line of Credit
By Anthony Hollis

Good financing is an essential part of running a business. But no bank loan comes automatically. How to get a Business Loan or Line of Credit shows you exactly what to do to get a Business Loan or a Line of Credit. This book is the ultimate resource for anyone starting and operation a business. A bank loan can provide the financial boost a business needs to add a product line or expand a market—or provide cash to take advantage of supplier discounts. This book, by Anthony Hollis, explains everything you need to know to get the credit you want.

National Charter School Developers Handbook: A Resource Guide for getting your Charter School off the ground.
By Anthony Hollis

This handbook, written by Anthony Hollis, provides potential charter school developers with practical advice for the essential phases of planning, designing, and operating a charter school. Guiding principles and tips for the following are included: drafting a charter proposal; gaining community support; developing an educational program and accountability standards; recruiting and enrolling students; designing a school governance structure; recruiting and selecting staff; making personnel policies and contracts; fundraising and budgeting; finding and financing facilities; and complying with laws that apply to charter schools.

How Community—Based Organizations can start Charter Schools
By Anthony Hollis

The emergence of the public charter school movement has contributed new energy and vitality to the emphasis on school-community collaboration. A growing number of charter schools are being designed, launched and operated by community-based nonprofit organizations. This guide addresses creating and sustaining a healthy relationship between a new charter school and a founding nonprofit, leading to the creation and operation of a highly successful school. The guide draws on the latest thinking about building effective partnerships and alliances. Several sample documents are included.

Anthony Hollis' Guide to starting your own business
By Anthony Hollis

Today's conditions are among the best in history for starting and building your own business, and the author Anthony Hollis is renowned for showing hundreds of entrepreneurs how to do just that. Now let this hands-on book give you the market-tested knowledge and confidence you need to identify and evaluate new business opportunities, find money to get your new business venture off the ground, and take that first step toward true success-by launching a business that you know will work.

Starting a nonprofit organization for your church
By Anthony Hollis

If you are thinking about starting a nonprofit at your church, this book is an invaluable resource. A large and growing number of congregations are setting up church-based nonprofit organization in order to operate community development or educational programs. Once formed, the nonprofit structure allows for new opportunities for accessing additional funding and drawing new collaborative partners and volunteers into the ministry. Anthony Hollis outlines the step-by-step procedures for setting up a 501(c) (3) nonprofit organization connected to a congregation using simple, easy-to-understand terminology.

To receive more information about Anthony's seminars, products, and services, write:

Anthony Hollis
8879 W Colonial Dr Suite 153
Ocoee, FL 34761

0-595-33821-6

Printed in the United States
35607LVS00005B/133-135

9 780595 338214